Arnold Swanberg
September 19, 1987

Douglas A-4 Skyhawk

602
RESCUE
AB
144628
NAVY

OSPREY AIR COMBAT

Douglas A-4 Skyhawk

Peter Kilduff

Published in 1983 by Osprey Publishing Limited
12-14 Long Acre, London WC2E 9LP
Member company of the George Philip Group

Sole distributors for the USA

Osceola, Wisconsin 54020, USA

British Library Cataloguing in Publication Data

Kilduff, Peter
Douglas A-4 Skyhawk. – (Osprey air combat)
1. Skyhawk bomber – History
I. Title
623.74'64 TL686.D65
ISBN 0-85045-529-4

Originated and produced by
Anchor Books Limited, Bournemouth, Dorset

Photosetting by Poole Typesetting (Wessex) Limited, Bournemouth, Dorset
Page Film by Aero Offset (Bournemouth) Limited, Bournemouth, Dorset
Colour separations by Apperley Graphics Limited, Parkstone, Dorset
Printed in England by
BAS Printers, Over Wallop,
Hampshire

Contents

Acknowledgements

During the spring of 1961, the aircraft carrier USS *Lake Champlain* (CVS-39) was host to friendly ranking naval officers from throughout Central and South America for an impressive firepower display off Roosevelt Roads, Puerto Rico. A highlight of the event was a demonstration of the loft bombing technique with which the relatively new Skyhawk series was to deliver tactical nuclear weapons. That demonstration, witnessed and never forgotten by this writer, led to an abiding interest in the Skyhawk that eventually resulted in this book.

Thanks to a number of helpful people and the perserverance of my publisher, Jasper Spencer-Smith, this operational history of the Skyhawk has become a reality. Rear Admiral Robert E. Kirksey, an A–4 pilot with considerable combat experience, was extremely helpful in sharing his own experiences and introducing me to some of his contemporaries with related experiences.

My sincere thanks go to these very helpful people for providing assistance with this book: Dr D.C. Allard, Head, Operational Archives Branch, Naval Historical Center; the Blue Angels flight demonstration team; Robert A. Carlisle, Head, Still Photo Branch, Office of Information; Rear Admiral Bryan W. Compton Jr, USN (Ret); Danny J. Crawford, Head, Reference Section, US Marine Corps History and Museums Division; John R. Dailey, Public Relations Director, Lockheed Aircraft Service Company; Harry S. Gann, Manager, Aircraft Information, Douglas Aircraft Company; Roy A. Grossnick, Historian, Naval Aviation History Office; Edward H. Heinemann, leader of the A-4 design team and known throughout US naval air facilities as Mr Attack Aviation; Admiral James L. Holloway III, USN (Ret), former Chief of Naval Operations; JOl David Kronberger, US Navy Office of Information; Robert L. Lawson, editor of *The Hook*, quarterly magazine of The Tailhook Association; Edward J. Leary, a friend whose background in aeronautical engineering was helpful in translating some of the technical material for a wider audience; Harvey Lippincott, Corporate Historian and Archivist, United Technologies Corporation; the Royal Australian Navy's office of information; Flying Officer G.C. Stewart, Adjutant, 75 Squadron, RNZAF; First Lieutenant James Swofford, USMC; Rear Admiral E.E. (Gene) Tissot, USN (Ret); Anna C. Urband, Assistant Head, Media Services Branch, US Navy Office of Information; Clarke Van Vleet, Historian Emeritus, US Naval Aviation History Office; and Major R.S. (Sam) Williams, USMC, of the US Naval Air Test Center. Special thanks go to my literary 'co-pilot', my wife Judy, whose powers of proof-reading and reasoning were essential to the orderly completion of this work.

Peter Kilduff
New Britain, Connecticut
April 1983

Foreword

Many words have been written about the Douglas A-4 Skyhawk series and, in view of its popularity, I expect that more will be written in the years to come. In this operational history of the Skyhawk, author Peter Kilduff tells the story with emphasis on the pilot's view, quoting some of the officers who saw the Skyhawk through the war in south-east Asia and elsewhere.

My own cockpit view of the Skyhawk came about in February 1974, when Vice Admiral Bill Houser, then Deputy Chief of Naval Operations (Air Warfare), arranged for me to take a ride in a TA-4. That very fine gentleman knew how much it would mean to me to go up in the product of the design team I had led. Lieutenant Bill Mocock flew the aircraft out of NAS Miramar and out towards Catalina. Out over the water, he let me fly the plane and I found it a most pleasing experience.

When a new aircraft is developed, there is always great speculation as to its success if called upon to defend the nation. Will it meet its performance requirements? Will it fly well? And, most of all, will it be well received by the pilots whose ability to fight and whose lives will depend on it?

The answers to those questions are not apparent unless the aircraft is tested in combat. The condition of the world was such that the A-4 was called upon many times and was always ready when needed.

The A-4 was conceived 32 years ago and many examples are still going strong today. That's a great tribute to the men and women who designed and built it, and the people who flew it and maintained it.

To all of them I wish to say thank you for a job well done.

Edward H. Heineman
Rancho Santa Fe, California
March 1983

1
The Beginning

The Douglas Aircraft Company's A–4 Skyhawk jet-powered attack aircraft is one of the few modern aircraft to become a legend within its own rather long lifetime. Indeed, that long service life has given the legend ample time to develop, while continued use a quarter of a century after production began offers newer pilots the opportunity to verify the Skyhawk's legendary characteristics.

Never known as an 'easy' aircraft to fly, the Skyhawk has nonetheless earned the respect and gratitude of several generations of young pilots whose survival during hazardous missions can be attributed to the unique design and strength of this diminutive and lightweight ship-based aircraft.

No gathering of present or former Skyhawk pilots disperses without at least one affectionate tribute to the A–4 series. Rear Admiral Robert E. Kirksey, now a senior planner in the American defence network, is typical of the naval aviators who grew to admire and respect the Skyhawk. A highly decorated veteran of A–4 combat operations during the Vietnam War, Admiral Kirksey easily remembers 15 or more years earlier in his career when his 'office' was the narrow confines of a Skyhawk pilot's seat:

'The cockpit is relatively small, even for a person who, like myself, is not very tall, but it is also a very convenient cockpit, with everything in front of you. The "stick" just becomes an extension of your right hand and the throttle is very convenient to your left hand. With its small, bullet-type nose, it is as if you are sitting in a little capsule, looking out with a clear, unobstructed view through an arc of about 250 degrees. Visibility aft is poor, so you are looking primarily out on the forward hemisphere.

Douglas test pilot Robert Rahn flew the first XA4D-1 Skyhawk (BuNo 137812), on 22 June 1954. That event took place only 18 months after the detailed engineering work had been initiated. The X designation was subsequently dropped and the aircraft was later used as the mock-up for succeeding versions

'But when you roll – and the aircraft has a roll rate of 720 degrees per second – it is like going down a ski slope and getting quite a sweep of everything in sight. It is a good feeling. Exhilarating, in fact. Not that you go around "rolling" the airplane at every opportunity, but you have a lot of flexibility. The man and the machine are almost perfectly interfaced.

'The A–4 is not an inherently stable aircraft, so you have to "fly" the airplane all of the time. When you set it up on a glide slope to come aboard the carrier, you have to work the power and the lateral controls, all of which are very responsive. But it is not an aircraft in which you can trim it up, lock the friction knob on the throttle and then just come aboard at a good rate of descent, responding to power if you are in trouble.

'When you are aboard ship, watching the A–4 come in for a landing, it is almost like watching a little sparrow coming in to land on a tree limb. It is a little bit wobbly and the long landing gear seems to be reaching down to grasp the flight deck. But if you are a A–4 pilot, you know that a careful, measured approach, with continuous fine tuning, is just what it takes. As aviators, the people who fly the A–4 grow very fond of it, and all of the airplane's nuances become part of the people who fly it.'

The company that built the A-4 was founded by Donald Wills Douglas, who went into business for himself on 22 July 1920 after serving as chief engineer for American aviation pioneer Glen L. Martin. From the outset, Douglas had a strong connection with the US navy. A graduate of the US Naval Academy, Douglas went on to earn a bachelor's degree in the new field of aero engineering at Massachusetts Institute of Technology. In 1914, he became MIT's first instructor in aviation. Donald Douglas' brief career with Martin, from 1916 to 1920, convinced him that aviation would be one of the most promising careers of the 20th century. Thus, with financial backing from wealthy sportsman David R. Davis, he set up the Davis-Douglas Aircraft Company. The firm's first order was for a tough, clean sporting biplane for Davis' own use. The Cloudster, as it was

A4D-2 in flight showing the vortex generators added to the outboard leading edge of the wings to improve the lift by eliminating turbulence

called, turned out to conform almost exactly to the specifications for a new torpedo bomber that the US Navy wanted for its fast growing post-war air fleet. Consequently, when new financing resulted in the formation of the Douglas Aircraft Company, the firm won a contract to produce the Douglas DT–1. Under the system then in use, the designation signified the aircraft was a Douglas-

built Torpedo aircraft and the *first* of the type produced by that firm for the Navy.

Only one DT–1 was built, but the production model DT–2 marked the beginning of a long successful line of naval aircraft leading up to the Skyhawk series. A few years later, in 1927, the Douglas staff was increased by the hiring of a young draughtsman, Edward H. Heinemann, who would ultimately be responsible for the design and development of 23 Douglas aircraft and gain lasting prominence as the creator of the Skyhawk.

Edward Heinemann was born on 14 March 1908 in Saginaw, Michigan. The son of a Swiss-born mother and an American father of German descent, the future aircraft designer was christened Gustave Henry Heinemann. His early years were spent in an area of the United States noted for its German ethnic concentration and so he found himself one of many boys bearing the popular name of Gustave. He therefore displayed his strong will early in life by insisting on being called by the more distinctive name of Edward.

In 1915, the Heinemann family moved to California, where young Edward got his first exposure to aviation. The Panama Pacific International Exposition was then taking place and an attraction of the event was a display of flying by Art Smith and Lincoln Beachey, two pioneer American aviators.

Eventually, the family moved to Rogers Park, outside Los Angeles. While living there, Edward Heinemann was accepted at Manual Arts High School, a vocational training institute to prepare young men for work in various skilled trades. Among the other alumni of Manual Arts High is Lieutenant General James H. Doolittle, famed aeronautical engineer, air racer and leader of the first B–25 raid on Tokyo. At the vocational school Heinemann gained basic knowledge in the areas of drafting, electrical engineering, pattern making, machine operation, sheet metal work and forging – all of which were to be important when all-metal aircraft became more prominent.

Edward Heinemann did not complete his studies at Manual Arts High. 'During the summer of 1925, he wrote in his autobiography, I decided not to return to school. It wasn't that I was bored with the books. Rather, I felt an instinctive urge to apply what I had learned to a real job.' Likewise, he did not complete studies for a degree from an institution of higher learning. It can best be said that Edward Heinemann attended and benefitted from the 'University of the Mind', learning important new skills and knowledge through his association with a number of talented people.

He took night courses in aircraft design taught by Don Berlin, an engineer at Douglas Aircraft. He subsequently joined that company as a draughtsman, working on tracings and drawings for early Douglas military aircraft. There he met James H. ('Dutch') Kindelberger, later President of North American Aviation Inc, and also worked a desk away from Gerald F. Vultee, later a noted designer for Lockheed before forming his own company. While working on the successor to the Douglas DT–2, the T2D–1 (Torpedo aircraft, the second to be provided to the navy by Douglas, of which this was variant No 1), Heinemann's supervisor was John K. Northrop. Northrop subsequently went on to form his own company, whose experiments with flying-wing and delta designs provided useful information for Heinemann when later he developed the F4D Skyray and A4D Skyhawk aircraft.

The design simplicity of the A4D allowed airframe production to be divided into three major areas: forward fuselage (seen here), aft fuselage, and wing. All necessary equipment was built into each major component, so that, at the end of the production line, the aircraft could be quickly assembled

The early days of the American aviation industry were marked by highs and lows of productivity. At one low point, Heinemann left Douglas to gain further experience with other companies, but by January of 1932, he was back at Douglas, working for Jack Northrop at the plant in El Segundo. Work on the Northrop Gamma and Delta monoplanes, under an arrangement in which Donald W. Douglas owned 51 percent of the Northrop operation and could draw on its resources, led to development of the Northrop XFT–1, an experimental fighter aircraft for the US Navy. Edward Heinemann worked on the XFT–1, its successor, the Model 3A, and then the XBT–1 torpedo bomber.

By 1936, Heinemann was chief engineer of the El Segundo Division, in which position he influenced the long line of Douglas military aircraft produced during World War II and beyond. There is a logical evolution of these types, culminating in the A4D. From the TBD-1 onward, the aim was to produce the strongest aircraft, capable of carrying maximum ordnance or firepower to enemy positions with the best possible performance to assure both aircrew protection and the ability to penetrate enemy air defences. A tall order, to be sure, but one met by a successful series of torpedo – or bomb-carrying attack aircraft, which included the SBD Dauntless dive bomber for the US Navy and the A-20 Boston/Havoc, A-24 Dauntless and A-26 Invader attack bombers for the US Army Air Corps (later the US Air Force).

Heinemann's fine hand is evident in the SB2D and BT Destroyer aircraft, TB2D Devastator torpedo bomber and, after World War II, the D-558-1, Skystreak jet reasearch aircraft and the D-558-2 Skyrocket rocket-powered research aircraft, the latter being the first aircraft to attain twice the speed of sound.

Certainly one of the most notable aircraft to come out of the Heinemann design team was the Douglas AD Skyraider series of carrier-based attack aircraft. Designed for service in World War II, the 'Able Dog' went on to serve in the Korean and Vietnam Wars, the latter being marked by transfer of US Navy ADs to the US Air Force for their use in counter-insurgency operations.

The AD Skyraider series was, however, a propeller-driven aircraft and in the years following World War II there was ever greater emphaisis on developing carrier-based jet-powered fighter and attack aircraft. In the former category, the Douglas F3D Skyknight was developed by Heinemann's team to meet the Navy's requirement of a two-place dedicated nightfighter to afford Fleet protection

The A4D cantiliver low wing had a modified delta planform with a 33-degree sweep. Wing spars were machined in one piece from solid stock and were continuous from wingtip to wingtip, thereby adding strength to the design. The three wing spars formed a box that proved to be an ideal integral fuel tank (so-called 'wet wing') to give added range to the Skyhawk series

at all hours and to be able to interdict the enemy ashore under cover of darkness. In that role, it was an early success. Similarly, the supersonic Douglas F4D Skyray was an impressive highly manoeuvrable delta-winged ship-based fighter (it's successor, the F5D Skylancer, offered even more promise, but was simply never ordered into production).

The problem, however, was in finding a jet-powered successor to the AD series. The proposed A2D Skyshark turboprop-powered attack bomber was beset with operational problems centering on the aircraft's complex gearbox to accommodate the two contra-rotating propellers. The successful A3D Skywarrior was a carrier-based *heavy* attack aircraft not at all intended for AD Skyraider-type missions. The obvious solution was to develop an entirely new aircraft, powered by a pure jets rather than turboprops.

Heinemann found the opportunity to propose a solution during a January 1952 meeting with officials of the US Navy's Bureau of Aeronautics (abbreviated BuAer) in Washington, DC. Heinemann and Robert Canaday of Douglas' Washington office had scheduled a meeting with the Chief of BuAer, Rear Admiral Thomas S. Combs, to discuss ways of holding down the weight and cost of the new generation of jet-powered aircraft then entering Fleet service. Admiral Combs was unable to attend the meeting, but was represented by Rear Admiral Apollo Soucek, a record-setting pilot in the 'biplane navy' of the late 1920s who went on to command Task Force 77 during part of the Korean War. Admiral Soucek, who subsequently became Chief of BuAer, was intrigued by Heinemann's outline of a light-weight interceptor that would reverse the trend of heavier, costlier jet-powered aircraft.

He began by aplty citing the need for the aircraft, as the outline was not then part of the Navy's proposed plans for aircraft acquisition: 'If equipment', Heinemann told the ranking officers and civilian experts present, 'and performance is to remain constant, then the wing area, power plant, fuel and structure must be increased by as much as 100 percent. This growth factor of ten depends on the type of aircraft, but is a reasonably accepted average. (Conversely) . . . if you increase weight at the sacrifice of performance, you cheat the pilot and you have a poorer aircraft'.

Heinemann was reminded that previous plans for a naval interceptor had already been cancelled, implying there was no need to match the one he was explaining. But then Soucek asked whether Heinemann's growth factor would apply as well to a jet-powered light-attack bomber. Heinemann said it would and the Admiral shot back to question the realistic weight of such an aircraft. '12,000 pounds', Heinemann responded. While some of the Navy people present chuckled at the low weight proposed, Souceck asked for a working concept he could take the higher naval authorities.

Challenged to demonstrate how Douglas could provide a low-cost jet-powered light-attack aircraft. Heinemann and his group returned to El Segundo to begin serious work on the project. Primary consideration was given to weight-saving aspects of the new design. Thus, the short-span wing of 27 feet 6 inches not only made it possible to save 200 pounds of metal, but also eliminated the wing folding mechanism required of most other carrier-based aircraft. In turn, this delta-wing planform allowed for a single-unit wing construction, a so-called 'wet-wing' that could accommodate a 560-gallon (US) fuel tank in addition to the 240-gallon (US) tank in the fuselage. The result was added savings in the reduced number and weight of necessary fuel valves and pipes.

Most modern aircraft feature some redundancy in controls to give the pilot a back-up in the event of one system failing. Heinemann's team was able to eliminate one hydraulic system by designing the landing gear so that it retracted *forward* to lie in fairings below the wing surface, with the wheels turning through 90 degrees to lie flat in apertures forward of the main structure. Thus, in case of hydraulic system failure, the landing gear could be released and forced into the 'down' position by the airflow. Also in cases of hydraulic system failure, the control column could be extended approximately 12 inches to allow the pilot greater leverage in working the controls manually.

Further weight savings were achieved by designing the fuselage with a single transport joint. Thus, the fuselage 'broke' in the middle, at a point where the frame portion supporting the engine was bolted to the intermediate spar of the wing. This system also allowed for quicker engine changes, as the airplane literally 'broke' into two parts for immediate and complete access to the powerplant.

As the project developed, other less-complex and weight-saving ideas were introduced: an on-board air conditioning system that was 25 pounds lighter than that in other aircraft, a consolidated avionics package that saved another 40 pounds and a totally new ejection seat system that weighed 40 pounds versus 98 pounds for the standard model.

To reinforce the challenge, Heinemann had a sign placed over the door of his office bearing the legend: 'If it's: less weight, more gas, simple design, better quality, improved take-off, less gingerbread, better performance, COME IN; as a matter of fact, we're glad to have you!

The entire Douglas design team and the company's suppliers of related components rose to the challenge and ultimately came up with a design that was five pounds lighter than the goal Heinemann had set. Unfortunately, the Navy had a few other – newer – requirements that affected the final weight of the aircraft, and these simply

The 'Blue Blasters' VA-34 flying in squadron formation

LEFT
Two A4D-1s of the 'Blue Blasters' VA-34 fly in formation during a 1957 training exercise. Later, VA-34 became the first Skyhawk squadron to earn Navy E awards for operational efficiency. During a deployment to NAS Leeward Point, Cuba, 'Blue Blasters' pilots scored 22 Es in three competitive exercises covering over-the-shoulder, loft and high-altitude bombing. Ensign I. D. Lewey, pilot of the A4D-1 in the background (BuNo 139963), won an E for loft bombing

had to be accommodated. Admiral Soucek informed Ed Heinemann (as he prefers to be called) that the aircraft would have to have a 2,000-pound bomb capacity and use JP type jet fuel, which weighed approximately half a pound per US gallon more than the same amount of conventional aviation gasoline. ($6\frac{1}{2}$ vs 6 lbs/gal).

The fine points were worked out and the new Douglas light attack aircraft – designated A4D – was on its way to becoming a reality. On 21 June 1952, the US Navy issued a contract for two prototype aircraft to meet some very rigid specifications: maximum speed of 500 mph, 460-mile operating radius, 2,000lb bomb capacity – and, most important, the aircraft had to be produced for an absolute maximum cost of $1 million per copy. As it turned out, the speed requirement was exceeded and the first 500 aircraft were delivered at a cost of some $860,000 each.

By the following October, the A4D design had been evaluated by the Navy's mock-up board, further alterations were suggested and two contracts for 19 pre-production aircraft were authorised. The Douglas plant in El Segundo began gearing up to produce the aircraft, a process that led to further refinements. In producing the wings, for example, by making the spars in one piece and bending them as needed to fit their respective positions, they formed a better, lighter structure less likely to leak fuel.

The XA4D-1 made its first flight on 22 June 1954, with Douglas test pilot Rob Rahn at the controls. The first aircraft, assigned the BuAer serial number 137812, was powered by a Curtiss-Wright J65-W-2, a licence-built Armstrong-Siddeley Sapphire engine that developed 7,200lb of thrust. The production models were

A4D-1 of the 'Challengers' VA-43 lands aboard the training aircraft carrier USS *Antietam* (CVS-36) in 1960. NAS Oceana-based VA-43 was one of two Skyhawk squadrons offering instrument training (the other was VA-45) and included operations aboard USS *Antietam*, the first American carrier to be fitted with an angled flight deck. *Antietam* served as the training carrier until she was decommissioned in May 1963 and succeeded in that role by USS *Lexington* (CVS-16)

equipped with the 7,800lb thrust J65-W-4 and -4B variants, which came mainly from stocks of reconditioned engines used in US Air Force Republic F-84F Thunderstreak jet fighters.

Early tests with the XA4D-1 revealed buffeting at certain speeds. That condition was corrected by adding the so-called 'sugar scoop' over the tail pipe to smooth out the airflow. Vortex generators, 11 small metal tabs, were added to the tops of the leading edges of both wings near the tips to improve wing lift by eliminating turbulence. And the smooth rudder structure was significantly altered to eliminate 'buzz' or high-frequency, low-amplitude flutter of the rudder panel. The latter modification was made by applying a correction originally made to the North American FJ-4 Fury, in which the rudder surface was turned inside-out, with the supporting ribs on the outside and the smooth metal on the inside. This so-called 'tadpole section' was developed on the A4D-1, but became standard on succeeding models.

Douglas' flight testing was succeeded by a series of tests made by the Naval Air Test Center (NATC) at the US Naval Air Station in Patuxent River, Maryland. NAS Patuxent River, which is also home for the US Navy Test Pilot School, generally sees every US Navy and Marine Corps aircraft intended for Fleet service. The facility has its own simulated flight deck, with both steam-powered catapult equipment and arresting gear. Aircraft slated for shipboard use are first extensively tested at NATC's own facility and then taken to sea for Carrier Suitability Trials, which, in the case of the A4D-1, were carried out in September 1955 aboard USS *Ticonderoga* (CVA-14).

On 15 October 1955, Lieutenant Gordon Gray of the Navy test team set a new 500-kilometer closed-course world speed record in the second production model A4D-1 (BuNo 137814). Although fitted with the less-powerful J65-W-2 engine, Gray's aircraft was clocked at 695·163 miles per hour at an altitude of 100 metres (328 feet) at Edwards Air Force Base in California. The previous record had been set by a North American F-86H Sabre jet fighter and the A4D's flight marked the first time that this particular record had been broken by an attack aircraft.

Due to its diminutive size, the A4D acquired a number of unofficial nicknames. 'Tinker Toy Bomber', 'Scooter', 'Bantam Bomber' and, perhaps most flattering of all to the driving force behind the aircraft, 'Heinemann's Hot Rod'. However, the name that has stuck with the series came from the first squadron to use the aircraft operationally, Navy attack squadron VA-72, whose nickname was the 'Hawks'. Originally a fighter squadron designated VF-72, the unit adopted the hawk as its insignia in 1946. Since the Douglas Aircraft Company was to use the prefix 'sky' on all its post-World War II aircraft (Skyraider, Skystreak, Skyrocket, Skynight, Skyshark, Skywarrior, Skyray and Skylancer), it was easy for the formal name Skyhawk to arise from the readily adaptable nickname of the first operation A4D-1 squadron (interestingly enough, a short time later – and while still operational with A4D aircraft – VA-72 changed its nickname to the 'Blue Hawks').

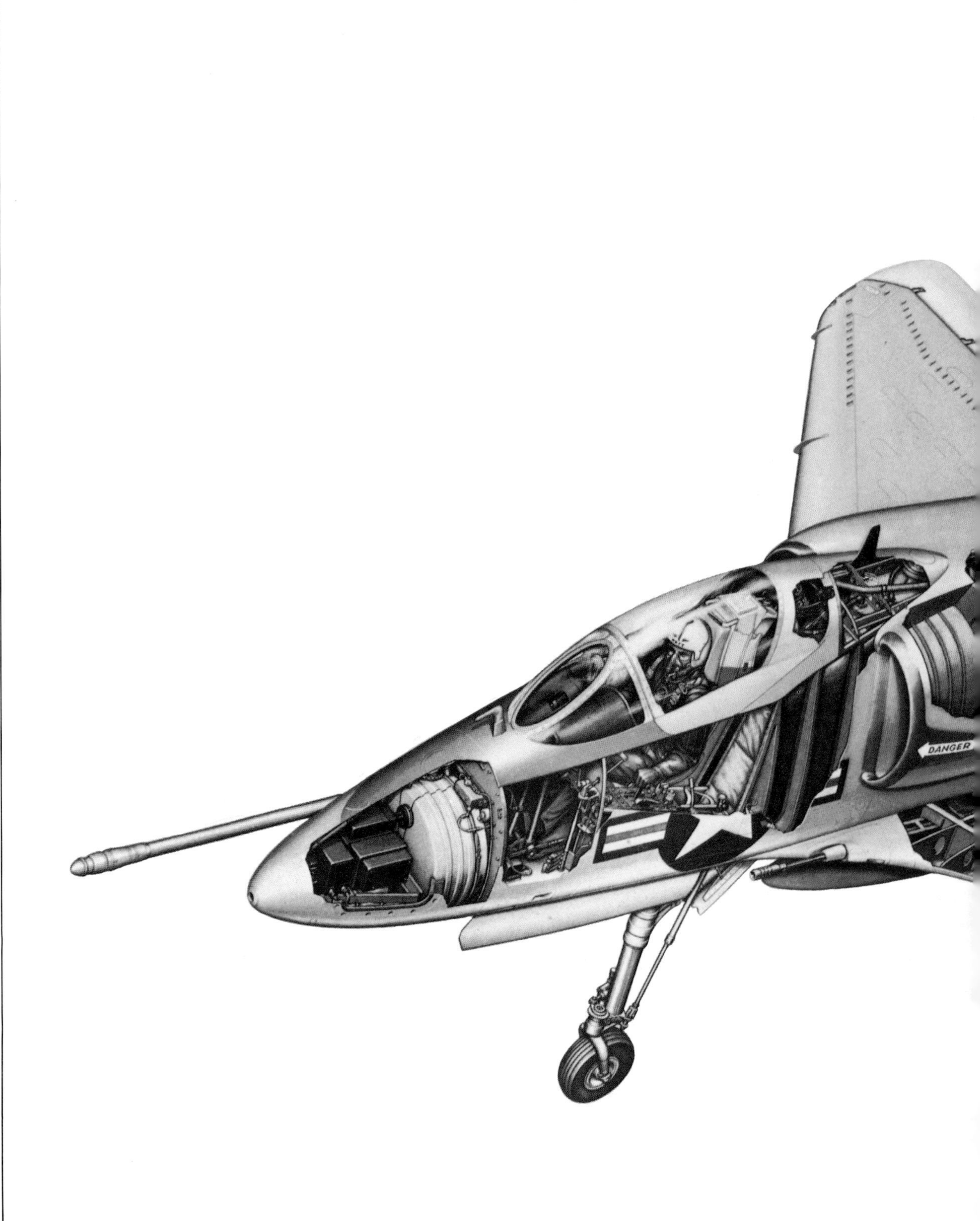
DANGER

Cutaway view of the A4D-2 shows the compactness of the aircraft, from the radar gear in the nose to the durable wing construction and close fit of the aft fuselage section around the engine

NAVY
142853

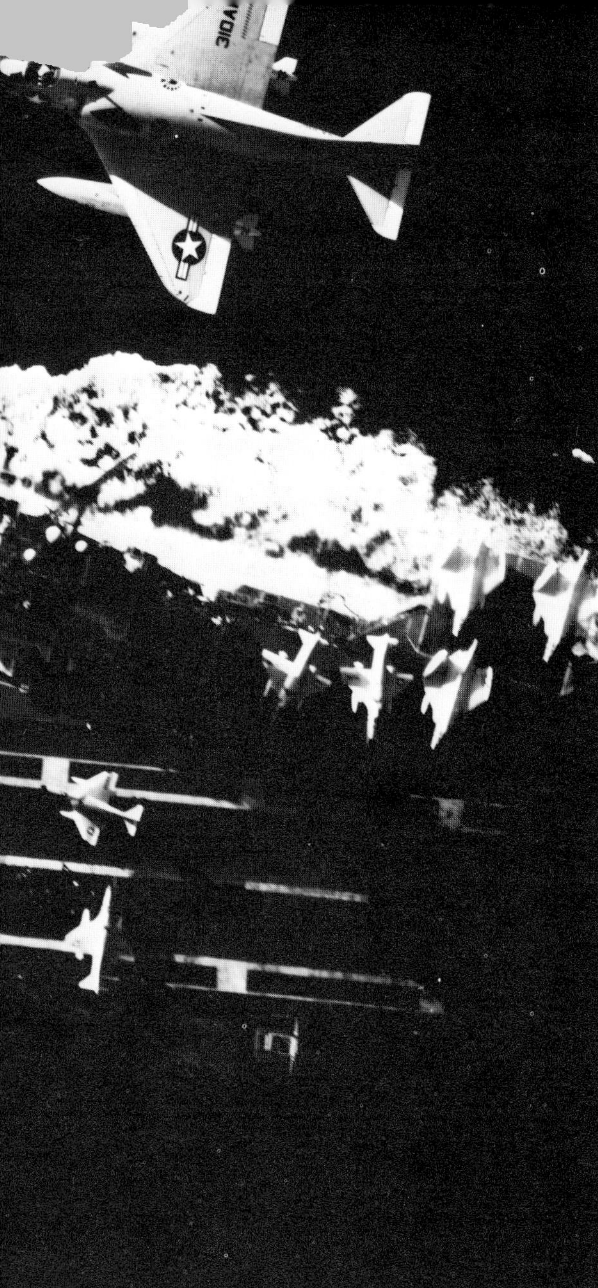

The 'Gladiators' VA-106 fly in formation over USS *Shangri-La* (CVA-38) during 1962 Mediterranean deployment

BELOW LEFT
In profile, the A4D-2 shows the tadpole rudder and the sugar scoop tailpipe fairing, both devised to improve the Skyhawk's performance. The A4D-2 also introduced the long, straight refuelling probe on the starboard side of the aircraft

BELOW
As part of the early refinement of the Skyhawk series, this A4D-1 was used by the Naval Aviation Ordnance Testing Facility at Chincoteague, Virginia. Tests were carried out at other Navy facilities and by Douglas as part of a continuing programme to make the best use of what was then the Navy's most diminutive jet-powered attack aircraft

VA-72, then based on NAS Quonset Point, Rhode Island, began receiving A4D-1s on 9 September 1956. The squadron had previously been equipped (as a figher squadron) with Grumman F9F-5 Panther jets of Korean War vintage. VA-72 then became responsible for the Fleet Introduction Program (FIP) for the Skyhawk, serving as a field training unit for selected US Navy and Marine Corps pilots. The new A4D-1 pilots were integrated into the familiarization syllabus, given ground training in the aircraft, demonstrations of its various components and then an initial series of flights.

The A4D-1 Skyhawk was officially declared operation on 26 October 1956. The following January, deliveries of A4D-1s were begun to the first Marine Corps squadron, VMA-224, based at MCAS El Toro, California. VMA-224 also converted from F9F-5s to the new light attack jets.

In the Pacific Fleet, VA-125 became the Replacement Air Group and, thus, the first operational West Coast A-4 squadron in the Navy. After completing their own convertion from the Grumman F9F-8 Cougar to the Skyhawk, VA-125 was assigned to train pilots and ground support crews of VA-93 on the new aircraft.

The operational 'ripple' effect had begun. More and more units gave up older aircraft (mostly jet-powered fighters) for the new product of Ed Heinemann's talented El Segundo operation. Towards that end, progress continued even as new units were re-equipping with Skyhawk. When VMA-211 received its Skyhawks in September of 1957, they were the new and improved A4D-2 variant. The first Navy squadron slated for the -2, VA-12, received the new aircraft while shore based at NAS Cecil Field, Florida.

Eventually, 18 Navy and Marine Corps squadrons operated all but one of the 166 A4D-1 aircraft built. The exception, the first test aircraft BuNo 137812, served as the mock-up for later versions. As events subsequently proved, the operational aircraft came on the scene just in time to begin showing that the Skyhawk would be all that Ed Heinemann promised Admiral Soucek it would be.

2

First Combat Operations

The first of the Skyhawk series entered Fleet service at a time of general international unrest. The American President at the time, Dwight D. Eisenhower, a retired five-star US Army general and national hero of World War II, had managed to conclude the Korean War – but only with an armistice, rather than a more permanent determination. In essence, hostilities could be resumed. Other moves by the Soviet Union and the People's Republic of China gave little comfort to the non-communist world. All of these events combined to convince President Eisenhower's chief foreign policy strategist, Secretary of State John Foster Dulles that the only sure way to keep the communist bloc nations at bay was to maintain a heavy political and military presence at the brink of war.

Given all these events, the US Navy had an early prominent role in America's atomic defence strategy. In the early 1950s, North American AJ–1 Savage aircraft of composite squadron VC–5 were held in readiness to deliver nuclear weapons after being launched from *Midway*-class carriers, which, at the time, were the largest aircraft carriers in the American defence arsenal. The Savage, powered by a piston engine on each wing and a jet engine in the tail, was only just adequate for the mission. The new Skyhawk, however, was ideally suited to the purpose and was publicly acknowledged as the US Navy's 'atom bomber'. Thus, it had an important early role in the way the United States waged the so-called 'Cold War' to keep the Soviets from sparking a hotter conflict, and, when Middle East instability threatened to go even further – following an abortive communist-inspired *coup d'etat* in

A4D-2 of the 'Sidewinders' VA-86, fitted with the standard two 400 (US) gallon long-range fuel tanks, ready for take-off on the starboard catapult of USS *Randolph* (CVA-15) during 1958 deployment. The aircraft shown is that of VA-86's commanding officer at the time, Commander W. A. Schroeder. The large E on the air intake, forward of the squadron insignia, indicates the squadron's attainment of Navy operational efficiency awards

Jordan and a successful *coup* in Iraq – the Skyhawk was sent in squadron strength for its first test under combat conditions.

When the Lebanese government feared the tide of leftist revolutionary activity was about to engulf it in 1958, it sought military support from Britain, France and the United States. The American response included A4D–1 and –2 Skyhawks of VA–83, then led by Commander James L. Holloway III, a former dive-bomber pilot and a highly decorated fighter squadron commander during the Korean War. Now a retired four-star officer whose 37-year military career had been capped by a tour of duty as the Chief of Naval Operations, the highest uniformed post in the US Navy, Admiral Holloway recalls VA-83's transition to the Skyhawk prior to the squadron's first cruise under combat conditions.

'When I took command of VA–83, the squadron was flying the Vought F7U–3M Cutlass. It was a very advanced aircraft for its time, being one of the first naval aircraft with afterburner. The F7U gave very good performance when everything was working; unfortunately, it was a complex airplane and very difficult to maintain in a fully operational status. Furthermore, it had a strong proclivity toward system failures in flight and, as a result, the plane had a fairly high accident rate. In instances of hydraulic systems failure, pilots had to eject from the aircraft because, with the hydraulic systems gone, there was no way to control the bird. Another bad feature was the very tall tricycle landing gear which gave serious consequences to an otherwise minor accident that might occur landing aboard ship.'

Operational problems led to the F7Us of VA–83 conducting a portion of their flight operations ashore during the squadron's 1956 Mediterranean cruise aboard USS *Intrepid* (CVA–11). Thus, when that twin-engine-with-afterburner aircraft was replaced by the A4D–1 with a single engine *without* afterburner, one might have expected an interesting reaction from the pilots of VA–83. Admiral Holloway recalls: 'The pilots were elated when we received information in the winter of 1956 that the

AB
2730
NAVY
401
AB
2724
NAVY
407

squadron would be assigned A4D-1 and be among the first squadrons to operate the new plane. Whereas our flight time in the F7U had been sporadic and minimal, with seldom more than four aircraft flying at one time to conduct tactics, the A4D opened a whole new vista in terms of pilot satisfaction.'

In the mid-1950s, naval aviation personnel understood that the A4D had been designed for the special mission of delivering tactical nuclear weapons. Indeed, there was a great deal of talk about early A4D designs having the nuclear device streamlined to complement the shape of the aircraft's fuselage. What emerged, however, was not a limited, single-mission aircraft. Rather, it turned out to be a versatile light-attack aircraft with a high thrust-to-weight ratio that could strike far inland and return to its aircraft carrier base.

'Between the time that the A4D concept was originated and the plane was delivered to our squadron,' Admiral Holloway notes, 'the philosophy on nuclear weapons had changed. The earlier concept of a free use of tactical nuclear weapons didn't last long and by the time the A4D reached the Fleet the use of it in "special weapons delivery" was only one aspect of the Skyhawk. It was also to be used for the various attack aircraft tasks.

'Even though nuclear weapons delivery was not our sole mission, it was a primary mission and we practised very hard at it. At that time there were no intercontinental or submarine-launched ballistic missiles. The SIOP – Single Integrated Operations Plan – for the delivery of the major nuclear strike against the Soviet Union, which was perceived as our enemy then just as it is our main adversary now, was for these weapons to be delivered by the Strategic Air Command bomber force and carrier-based attack aircraft. The carriers were a major element in the SIOP. In times of tension, when the US was generating its force capability to conduct a nuclear strike against the Soviet Union, carriers would move into position in the Pacific and in the Mediterranean to assume their role in the plan.'

Using the A4D to launch nuclear weapons posed problems in assuring the accuracy of the delivery, which meant the pilot had to bring the aircraft fairly close to the target, and in assuring enough passage of time prior to detonation so that the pilot would be clear of the blast area. As Admiral Holloway points out, four basic methods were developed for A4D pilots.

'High-altitude delivery: the pilot would initiate a dive attack from 35,000 feet or more, releasing the bomb at 20,000 feet and then flying away to gain safe separation distance between the plane and the blast.

'Idiot loop: the pilot would come in very low at high speed and, when directly over the target, pull up to a steady 4g Immelmann. The on-board computer in the aircraft would release the bomb as the plane passed

Formation of A4D-2 Skyhawks of the 'Clansmen' VA-46 while attached to carrier air group CVG-1 in September 1958. CVG-1 subsequently went to sea aboard USS *Franklin D. Roosevelt* (CVA-42)

through about 90 degrees of the pull-up manoeuvre. The bomb would continue up to 12,000 feet and then fall on the target. Meanwhile, the aircraft would have completed the Immelmann and be scooting away from the target at maximum speed.

'Toss or loft bombing: again, the pilot would approach the target on a direct course. At a predetermined position known as the IP (initial point), the pilot would push his "pickle" (bomb release button) and the computer's timer would start. The pilot would continue to fly toward the target until his computer indicated the signal to pull up at a steady 4g rate. The bomb would be released after a computed pull-up of about 20 to 30 degrees, and it would then be 'tossed' or 'lofted' toward the target – a considerable distance, some 5,000 or 6,000 yards or more. After releasing the weapon, the pilot immediately executed a modified wing-over – a tightly-banked 180-degree turn – and dived down to the deck to gain maximum speed of escape.

'Lay-down: again, the aircraft penetrated at minimum altitude and very high speed – 50 to 150 feet at about 500 knots – to sneak in under hostile radar coverage. The technique was to get as close to the ground as possible and to fly directly over the target. The weapons used in this method were extremely rugged and, instead of being aerodynamically shaped, the nose was blunt, with a crown-shaped device we called a "cookie cutter". When the bomb was dropped, the cookie cutter kept it from bouncing along the terrain, which a streamlined bomb normally would do when dropped from very low altitude at high speed. With the cookie cutter in the nose, the bomb dug in to bring it to a sudden stop, and a timing device fired the weapon after enough of a delay to permit the aircraft to make good its escape.'

VA-83's acquisition of the new A4Ds and their special mission requirements was certainly a welcome change from the squadron's previous employment when operating the F7U Cutlass. Then, the F7U-3M (differing from other F7U-3s by having the capability of firing Sparrow air-to-air missiles) had as its normal routine a seemingly endless round of Combat Air Patrol (CAP) missions to protect the carrier and other aircraft in the assigned air wing.

With the arrival of the A4D, Admiral Holloway recalls, came a new and exciting schedule of air operations: 'At that time the squadron was based (in port) at the Oceana Naval Air Station in Virginia Beach, Virginia. "Sand blower" flight routes were laid out over unpopulated areas of Virginia and North Carolina, where we could train in low-level navigation. This legalized "flat-hatting" was great fun.

'So were the "idiot loop" and toss bomb manoeuvres. They were really authorised low-altitude aerobatics. We carried a load of eight small practice bombs to the bombing range. On each run we would accelerate to 500 knots. Over the target, we would pull up, maintaining as precisely as we could 4g on the accelerometer and very carefully keeping the wings level. If the plane's wings were not level, the bomb trajectory would be thrown off laterally. On these manoeuvres, we considered a miss distance of 500 feet not bad, regardless of how capable a bomber you were. In this kind of bombing there were uncontrollable factors, such as the wind, which is different at higher altitudes than at ground level. As the bomb was tossed through 12,000 feet, it would be affected by the

A4D-2 of the 'Waldomen' VA-66, then attached to carrier air group CVG-5, taxies forward prior to launch on routine training mission in 1959. A year earlier the squadron had converted from the Grumman F9F-8 Cougar

Instrument panel of the A4D-1 Skyhawk, the first variant flown by VA-83, shows the close grouping of controls that motivated early pilots to suggest a broader visual sweep of instrumentation, as found in subsequent models

different winds at all altitudes. Even with perfect technique, a bullseye was far from assured. They were really the result of luck as well as pilot skill.'

In addition to the entirely different mission schedule, pilots converting to the A4D encountered a number of other operational differences to be accommodated. The biggest difference was the size and roominess of the cockpit, since, without exception, the early A4D units had all been equipped with larger fighter aircraft. VA–72, the first unit to receive the A4D–1 in 1956, converted from the Grumman F9F–5 Cougar, as did VA–113 and VA–125 (F9F–8) later the same year. In 1957, VA–34 in F7U–3 and VA–83 in F7U–3Ms completed their re-equipment with A4D–1 aircraft. In 1958, VA–44 traded its F9F-8T training aircraft for A4Ds, to be used in the squadron's role as the Replacement Air Group (RAG) to train new pilots for the Fleet. That year, five other F9F–8 squadrons completed or initiated the A4D–1 conversion – VA–46, VA–66, VA–81, VA–106 and VA192 – as did one FJ–4 Fury squadron, VA–212. In succeeding years, four other FJ–4 units – VA–55, VA–94, VA–144 and VA–146 – made the change-over, as did three AD Skyraider squadrons – VA–15, VA–152 and VA–195.

For the former fighter aircraft pilots there was an initial adjustment to totally new cockpit equipment designed especially for the A4D–1 as part of Douglas' dedicated weight conservation effort. Standard shoulder harnesses were replaced by four buckles on the A4D–1 seat, fastened to a special torso harness worn by the pilot. Since the A4D–1 was one of the first US Navy aircraft to be equipped with liquid oxygen, pilots had to get used to new breathing equipment: a specially designed face mask with a torso harness-mounted regulator (instead of a cockpit-mounted regulator). The new torso harness and oxygen mask required a new life preserver in place of the standard 'Mae West' inflatable slip-on jacket; the new life preserver fitted around the pilot's waist so as not to interfere with the torso harness.

A4D-2 (A-4B) Skyhawks of the 'Sidewinders' VA-86 conduct inflight refueling during a Mediterranean training exercise in 1958. The lead aircraft (BuNo 142124) carries a centerline-mounted "buddy" store, at the forward end of which can be seen the spinning impeller of the wind-driven generator powering the pump to the transfer fuel to the recipient aircraft. During that cruise, the 'Sidewinders' were deployed aboard USS *Randolph* (CVA-15), seen cruising in the background

AG
2124
VA-86
NAVY
401

'One of the difficulties in introducing the A4D to the Fleet was that the new pilot's equipment had to come with the airplane,' Admiral Holloway remembers. 'We had some problems in that several of our pilots had unusual physiques and, as a consequence, their need for non-standard size equipment kept them from flying for a month or two after the plane arrived in the squadron. They had to wait until we could obtain torso harness that would fit them.

'There were also some "bugs" in the new oxygen masks and we found ourselves unable to fly high-altitude missions for several weeks. All of our masks had to go back to the factory for reworking.

'There are a lot of advantages to a totally new integrated aircraft systems concept in which everything is designed for that aircraft, from the pilot's gear to the aircraft support equipment, but it does become expensive. For one thing, each type of aircraft then has to have a unique support package. This leads to problems during the transition period, as new aircraft arrive slowly and, for a month or two, the squadron is flying the old aircraft as well as the new.'

As a case in point, Admiral Holloway cites the example of the A4D's mode of engine starting: 'A "huffer", a piece of rolling stock equipment that developed a blast of air, was used to spin a turbine at one end of a probe. The other end of the probe was inserted into the engine, where it was geared to spin the engine rotor assembly. Most other aircraft in the Fleet at that time had electrical starters and external electrical power was used to kick the starter over and get the engine going.

'Initially, we were using one starter probe per aircraft and they were always retained at the base. So, when we flew cross-country hops, we couldn't shut down our engines because there was no way to get them started again except at our home base.'

Some of the problems of the new aircraft were resolved by applying feedback from pilots to making improvements in succeeding variants, Admiral Holloway states: 'Several systems that were incorporated in the A4D–1 as new and streamlined approaches were not popular with the pilots and were eventually phased out when the A4D–2 came along. In the A4D–1, for example, the tailpipe temperature gauge registered only in the normal operating range – from about 450 to 550 degrees Fahrenheit.

'When the engine was at idle, if the instrument needle came off the peg at all, it didn't get up to where it registered on the gauge. This caused a definite problem on at least one occasion. One of our pilots was doing some test work at altitude and pulled the throttle back to the idle position for descent and thought he'd had a flame-out because the gauge needle wasn't registering. So he pulled the throttle all the way "around the horn", as it was called, to shut the engine down for an air-start and he *did* have a flame-out.

'He successfully re-started the engine, but as he came in for a landing, he again pulled the throttle back to idle and again thought he'd had a flame-out and therefore induced one by going through the flame-out air-start procedure. This was repeated several times. We were talking to him by radio and finally figured out what was happening. We convinced him that he still had a fire going when he had the throttle on idle, even though there was no indication on his gauges.

'We griped about this and were pleased to see that, when the A4D–2 came along, the tailpipe temperature gauge was calibrated all the way from 0 up to the maximum tailpipe temperature.

'The pilots also complained about the "idiot bars", their name for the oil temperature and pressure gauges, which either registered OK or displayed a striped hazard panel in the gauge window. The pilots felt this was an insult to their intelligence; they wanted to know what the pressure was – not just whether it was "go" or "no go". They felt that by noting the pressure and temperature they could better understand how the engine was performing. These gauges were also replaced with improved instruments in the A4D–2.'

The pilots of the early A4Ds often found themselves and their aircraft the objects of some good-natured humour at after-hours gatherings with pilots of other aircraft. The unusual design features – the low-mounted wing and the overall minimal size of the aircraft – were particularly noted. In the same good-natured spirit, members of VA–83 composed a song that proudly acknowledged some of the unique design aspects of the A4D. Sung to the tune of 'On the Street where You Live' from the Lerner and Loewe musical *My Fair Lady,* the ditty went like this:

People stop and stare,
Can't believe it's there.
It goes up and down
And 'round and 'round
And never gets nowhere.
Got no Omni gear,
Got no business here?
And it's known as the Ay-Four-Dee.

The reference to Omni gear was based on another aspect of the limited equipment found in the A4D–1. As Admiral Holloway notes: 'The only navigational equipment in the A4D–1 was TACAN (Tactical Air Navigation), which was and is an excellent system for ship-based use. In fact, the A4D–1 was one of the first aircraft to deploy with TACAN. But in those days, TACAN was not compatible with Omni, which is the navigational system for cross-country use within the United States. There were no TACAN stations within the domestic navigational network. Eventually, Omni and TACAN became compatible in their frequencies, but, prior to that, A4Ds on cross-country hops had to use visual means of navigation.'

Early in VA–83's operational life with the A4D–1 the squadron experienced incidents of engine failure that were not related to the engine idle problem previously noted. While the Naval Air Training and Operating Procedure Standardization (NATOPS) programme covered every conceivable aspect of aircraft operations in the weighty A4D NATOPS Manual that became the 'bible' of every pilot assigned to fly the aircraft, new information was added to the existing body of knowledge by the first few squadrons to operate an aircraft type. Thus, VA–83's

A4D-1 Skyhawks of VMA-224, the first US Marines Corps squadron to be equipped with the new attack aircraft. Photo taken in 1957 during early USMC operations

pilots had to cope with these engine failures as best they could, working with the Naval Air Systems Command (which runs the Naval Air Safety Center specifically to assure ongoing improvements in operational ability) and the engine manufacturer – Curtiss-Wright – to make corrections that would benefit all present and future A4D units.

Admiral Holloway recalls the first VA–83 incident: 'Ensign Bob Gonzalez experienced engine failure while he was conducting an "idiot loop". He attempted to eject, but the face curtain came out in his hands and the seat failed to fire, which was disconcerting. So he made a "dead stick" landing (without power) in a dried river bed near Guantanamo Bay, Cuba, where we were then conducting training operations. Bob received no injuries except some cactus stickers in his leg, which he picked up in abandoning the aircraft once it was on the ground.

'We continued to have engine failures. Fortunately, none of them resulted in crashes. On one occasion the engine quit while the plane was on the test track running up and, on another, an aircraft was taxi-ing back to its parking place on the flight line after a bombing hop when the engine failed. We found that all of these failures were occurring in the seventh stage blading of the compressor.

'As a consequence, the aircraft were grounded and we spent a week or so down in Guantanamo, waiting to be ungrounded, which did not happen. We simply received orders saying the planes were ungrounded for a one-time flight to our home base, where the engines would be exchanged for new or reworked units.

'When we returned to NAS Oceana, we learned that we would be deploying on 1 January 1958 with Air Task Group 201 to the Mediterranean for our normal six to eight months tour with the Sixth Fleet. Because ATG–201 was going out on a smaller deck *Essex*–class carrier – in fact, it was USS *Essex* (CVA–9) itself – we were to be equipped with the first A4D–2s. The –2 had in-flight refuelling equipment and there was concern that, with *Essex's* smaller flight deck, it would be more prone to flightdeck crashes and therefore it would be good if the aircraft could be refuelled as they "dogged" around the ship, waiting for the deck to be cleared. Not a very pleasant thought on which to begin a deployment and it was with considerable pride that we could subsequently report that, from the time we received the first A4D–2 until the end of the cruise, nearly a year later, we did not lose an aircraft. In fact, two blown tires were the extent of the operational damage to the planes during that deployment.'

Not all carrier based aircraft had a real all-weather operational capability at that time, but that fact did not diminish the US Navy's emphasis on the importance of an around-the-clock operational standard. Hence, night-time

A4D-1 (BuNo 142176) flown by Commander James L. Holloway, III, when the 'Rampagers' VA-83 first began operations with the Skyhawk. When the squadron made its 1958 deployment to the Mediterranean, however, it was equipped with the A4D-2

carrier flight operations were a routine part of most naval air exercises. Admiral Holloway points out, however, that night flying in early A4Ds led to suggestions for a number of improvements in later variants: 'The instrumentation was just not good enough. The flight instruments were located in the wrong part of the dashboard for good scan patterns. They were small and hard to see. The plane was very sensitive on the controls, which made it very hard to trim up and fly on instruments. You could gain or lose a thousand feet in the wink of an eye and, when you're flying at 500 feet, that could be fatal.

'Despite the problems, we really got our share of night flying in the A4D-2 during the warm-up period at NAS Jacksonville, Florida, prior to the cruise. An electrical problem led to the temporary grounding of all the McDonnell F2H-4 Banshees of VF-11, commanded by Commander Bill Allen, an Annapolis classmate of mine who was killed in a crash later in the cruise (19 August 1958) when his plane went into the water during a night

carrier landing. Because we needed jets airborne at night for training purposes, mainly for the ship's flight deck crews to get night aircraft deck handling training, the A4D-2s of VA-83 were pressed into service as night fighters. Our guys flew VF-11's missions and learned how to fly an A4D-2 off a carrier at night.

'Night-time carrier landing systems have improved greatly since 1958. In those days, the flight deck lighting was at an absolute minimum. There was a series of dim lights imbedded in the flight deck that showed the threshold and the center-line of the landing area, but they provided no illumination; they simply outlined the landing area.

'On a moonless night, with no horizon, the pilot would be flying only with reference to his cockpit instruments. As he rolled into the groove and picked up the "ball" (from the mirror landing system which established the glide path) in his descent to the carrier, he would look forward and try to pick out the dim deck lights. No doubt many of the accidents that did happen were caused by pilots attempting to make some sense out of the blur of indistinct lights – rather than continuing to fly on instruments, with only an occasional glance up at the deck to make sure it was still there.

'The destroyer astern of the carrier normally had its masthead light on and that one spot in the inky blackness was a point of reference. Theoretically, once you reached that point, you were lined up on the course on which you were supposed to land. Maintaining the proper altitude and speed to descend down the glide slope, the pilot lined up with the dim longitudinal lines on the flight deck and kept flying right onto the deck. When you heard a tremendous *Waang*! then you were aboard, hopefully, had engaged an arresting wire.

'The A4D-2 was a relatively short-coupled aircraft. That is, it was not particularly stable, either longitudinally or laterally. If the pilot became preoccupied looking out of the cockpit, the plane could be all over the sky in a few seconds – not where you'd want to be while trying to make a night-time landing. It was very difficult to trim up the airplane to fly it "hands off" down the glide slope. You were working all the time.'

Once USS *Essex* reached the Mediterranean, training exercises with the NATO allies began. The carrier-based aircraft of ATG-201 performed a range of missions. For example, they defended the task force against simulated hostile attacks by F-86 Sabres of the Italian Air Force. There were, however, special exercises for the A4D-2s of VA-83. Operational tactical nuclear weapons were brought out of the ship's magazines, checked out and loaded onto the aircraft.

'This was to ensure that we would be ready in case the real orders were given,' Admiral Holloway recalls. 'The nuclear weapons were much more complicated than the "iron bombs" we had normally used and required a great deal of testing, adjustment and checking out. When the nuclear weapons were hung on the aircraft, armed Marine sentries were placed on guard at each plane to keep unauthorized personnel from getting within ten feet of the weapon. That was done not so much to prevent sabotage as simply to keep the curious away.'

Obviously, nuclear strike operations were all to be carried out individually, with each aircraft assigned a specific target. Admiral Holloway describes a typical training mission in which the nuclear capable A4D-2s of VA-83 would fly in areas not far from the Iron Curtain countries that might reasonably be expected to be adversaries in any widespread military conflict.

'The pilots involved were called at about 0300 hours, and after an hour or so of final briefings, they spent considerable time in checking out the weapon on their aircraft. Once the weapons were determined to be in an "up" status, they were removed by the ordnance loading crew and returned to the ship's magazines. We never actually took off from the carrier on a training exercise with nuclear weapons loaded on the aircraft, but all other actual procedures were followed.

'With the weapons removed, the pilots manned their aircraft for launch and were catapulted into the black at about 0430 hours. This allowed arrival over their targets at the first light of day, as there was no capability in the A4D–2 at that time to attack targets under other than visual conditions.

'The A4Ds would be launched at five to fifteen-minute intervals, depending on where their targets were located. The objective was to coordinate carefully the times en route to the targets. On a typical mission, after take-off I climbed to 38,000 feet, my cruising altitude, and then proceed from the launch point south-east of the "boot" of Italy, up the Adriatic. To simulate a combat penetration of Central Europe.

'About 20 miles from landfall, my programmed flight route turned so there would be no inadvertent overflight of the unfriendly countries in that area. I flew a prescribed set of dog-legs over the Adriatic, replicating the actual flight profile in terms of altitude and speeds, but not, of course, in direction.

'At the proper point on the flight profile, about 50 miles from the target, I descended to minimum altitude for low-level navigation to the target, which was a rock in the water off the east coast of Italy. I then did my "idiot loop" manoeuvre and began my return to the carrier. Most of our flight profiles were flown at fairly long range, beyond the unrefuelled operating radius of the aircraft. Consequently, I had to rendezvous with a tanker aircraft, an AJ–2 Savage from the three-plane detachment of heavy attack squadron VAH–7 aboard *Essex*, and refuel in flight in order to make it back to the ship.

'I found the tanker where it was supposed to be, just off the "heel" of Italy, about 20 miles from the coast so that on a clear day we could confirm our navigation. The tanker was a welcome sight, making a big left-hand turn, just waiting for me. When he straightened out, I flew up behind hime and plugged in to the drogue at the end of a fuel hose being trailed by the tanker. I took on 1,000 pounds of fuel and, although I had room for more, that was all he could give me. He still had to fuel several other A4Ds coming home.

'After leaving the tanker, I continued my navigation to the carrier's position at high altitude to conserve fuel, as hostile detection was no longer a consideration. When I arrived the carrier was already steaming into the wind and I had the entire landing pattern to myself. I made a long, straight-in approach and came aboard with 600 pounds of fuel remaining and my mission accomplished by about 0715 hours.'

Just as ATG–201's exercises off the coast of Italy concluded, events in the Middle East began to heat up. President Nasser of Egypt was accepting vast shipments of Soviet arms and allowing his country to be used as a Soviet base of operations throughout the Middle East. Thus, when President Chamoun, the elected leader of Lebanon, found evidence of a *coup d'etat* in the making, he appealed

A4D-2 of the 'Flying Ubangis' VA-12 about to launch from the port catapult of USS *Forrestal,* (CVA-59) during, September 1959, refresher exercises in the Caribbean. USS *Forrestal,* the first of the large-deck super carriers, had just undergone its first shipyard overhaul

307

LTJG CHARLIE HUNTER
307

for outside help. The American government pledged to land a contingent of US Marines whose presence would free the Lebanese Army to pursue rebel forces in the country's interior. When the Marines landed, air groups from USS *Saratoga* (CVA–60) and USS *Essex* were to provide air cover.

Events were set in motion and the American naval force was deployed to Lebanon. That force was led by Admiral James L. Holloway Jr, USN, Commander-in-Chief, Middle East Specified Command, father of then Commander Holloway, skipper of VA–83. Despite stern warnings from Soviet Premier Khrushchev, who threatened to turn the Sixth Fleet aircraft carriers into 'flaming coffins' if an American landing was made, the operation took place without incident. Had the Soviet leader attempted to make good his threat, however, the American naval force would have been ready, as the younger Admiral Holloway recalls: 'VA–83 was required to keep one-third of our available aircraft rigged for nuclear weapons delivery. In fact, there were periods during the first day or two after the landings that the nuclear weapons were actually on the aircraft and checked out, with the Marine sentries on guard.

'The other two-thirds of our aircraft were employed on surveillance missions, which consisted mainly of flying border patrols around the perimeter of Lebanon, the Israeli as well as the Syrian side. We also conducted route reconnaissance, involving flying over some of the main roads leading out of the principal cities of Sidon, Tyre and Beirut and through the mountains into the Bekaa Valley and from there across the border. The purpose of the border patrols was to detect the incursion of any foreign military forces, and the road recces were just to keep track of what was moving on the roads in Lebanon.

'Normally, our planes carried full internal 20mm ammunition and two or four packs of 2·75-inch rockets. These could be fired in a salvo or semi-salvo or individually. These weapons were suitable for use against trucks, armoured vehicles or strongpoints. They were appropriate for the missions we were flying.'

With two American aircraft carriers on station off Lebanon, ATG–201 was able to stand down every fourth or fifth day, as squadrons from Carrier Air Group 3 aboard USS *Saratoga* flew all that day's missions. Likewise, ATG–201 would relieve CAG–3 squadrons for a replenishment stand-down. Even during non-flying days, the two air groups had to maintain aircraft at the ready, loaded and equipped for a fast reaction. There was also a fast-reaction group of nuclear-armed aircraft from VA–83, ready to go in the event an acknowledged 'nightmare scenario' became a reality. A4D–1s of VA–34 aboard *Saratoga* performed a similar function.

Commander James L. Holloway, III, commanding officer of VA-83 (right), presents an oversized replica of the Purple Heart decoration to Aviation Machinist's Mate T. E. Greer aboard USS *Essex* (CVA-9) following air operations over Lebanon in 1958. Greer was the plane captain (mechanic responsible for maintenance) for the A4D-2 flown by Lieutenant Robert G. Thomson (centre), which was struck by hostile ground fire. The real Purple Heart is presented to American military personnel wounded in action; hence, Lieutenant Thomson's A4D-1 was given this symbolic award

On two occasions during VA–83's four-week tour of duty off Lebanon, squadron aircraft came under hostile fire from the ground. Admiral Holloway remembers: 'In one case, Lieutenant (junior grade) "Butch" Swenson took a round through the wing of his A4D. The aircraft had a "wet wing" (full of fuel), which was not self-sealing. Consequently, when the wing took a hit, the fuel was pumped out rapidly by the pressurized fuel system.

'As soon as "Butch" assessed the damage, he headed for the carrier at 100 percent power. There was no point in trying to conserve fuel because he was in a race to get more fuel through the engine before it went through the hole in the wing.

'By the time he got back to the ship, he was down to 300 or 400 pounds of fuel, so he plugged in to a tanker. He took on only enough fuel to fill his fuselage tanks, thereby keeping what fuel he had from flowing out through the wing hole. He then had enough fuel to come aboard with an ample margin for a couple of wave-offs and "bolters" (attempted landings in which the arresting wire is not engaged).

'The second incident involved Lieutenant Bob Thompson, the squadron's operations officer. He took a round in the fuselage, near the cockpit. There was no critical damage to any vital components, so he was able to bring the plane back to the ship without difficulty.'

After the month-long operation, a US Air Force tactical fighter wing was transferred to the NATO base at Adana, Turkey. The two aircraft carriers were thus relieved of providing air support to the US Marine Corps ground forces. However, this action did not quickly end the first cruise for the A4D under hostile conditions. After leaving Lebanon for a much-deserved rest and recreation period in Italy, USS *Essex* and ATG–201 had been in Naples harbour only two days when they were ordered to weigh anchor and head for the Suez Canal.

The Chinese Communists were threatening to invade the offshore islands of Quemoy and Matsu, which had long been occupied by Chinese Nationalist forces. Consequently, the east coast-based USS *Essex* was detached from the Sixth Fleet in the Mediterranean and ordered to augment forces of the Seventh Fleet in the Western Pacific.

After passing through the Suez Canal and the Indian Ocean, the situation had changed, notes Admiral Holloway: 'By the time we got there, the most critical point of the crisis had passed and things were beginning to settle down. Nevertheless, we spent a lot of time at sea off the coast of mainland China, conducting intensive air operations at altitudes that would ensure that the Chinese radar units knew we were there.'

When USS *Essex* finally returned ATG–201 to the ship's home port in Mayport, Florida, 11 months after departure, it marked the end of a cruise in which the carrier had steamed more than 75,000 miles and had shown the flexibility of the A4D to respond to crises both present and nearly present in two hemispheres.

3
Developments

In 1954, the year the XA4D–1 made its first flight, Ed Heinemann received one of the most prestigious American aviation honours. He was a co-winner of the Collier Trophy, presented annually for the greatest American aviation achievement of the year. The award was personally presented by US President Dwight D. Eisenhower to Heinemann for his work on the F4D Skyray fighter and to his old friend and mentor 'Dutch' Kindelberger for his work on the North American F–100 Super Sabre jet fighter. Although never recognised to such a high formal degree, in its way the A4D project would go on to surpass both the F4D and the F–100 in the value it provided to aviation of the non-communist world. For one thing, the 2,960 A–4 and TA–4 Skyhawks built during a 26—year period from 1953 to 1979 form a production longevity chain unmatched in the history of US military aviation.

Throughout the long production run the Skyhawk was the subject of continual improvement and adaption to new requirements. While the A4D–1 was still in production, improvements for the A4D–2 and its successors were being developed, either by Douglas or at the instigation of the Navy.

Early in the production run Ed Heinemann was in Baltimore, Maryland on company business when one suggestion was advanced by senior Captain (already selected for appointment to rear Admiral) Thomas H.

Two A-4Cs of the 'War Eagles' VSF-1 are flanked by A-4Cs of the 'Spirits' VA-76 aboard USS *Independence* (CVA-62). On 1 April 1967, a detachment of VSF-1 was enlarged and formed the second full-fledged ASW fighter squadron, VSF-3. It was assigned to CVW-10 aboard USS *Intrepid* (CVS-11), to perform a limited attack role during the Vietnam War. In that period VSF-3 used A-4B aircraft brought out of retirement or procured from the Naval Air Reserve. They dropped over one million pounds of ordnance in the normal A-4 attack manner but did not fly the fighter-type missions that led to the squadron's designation

Moorer. A highly experienced naval aviator, Moorer (who was subsequently advanced to Chief of Naval Operations and then Chairman of the Joint Chiefs of Staff) asked Heinemann to develop an in-flight refueling tanker capability for both the A3D Skywarrior and A4D Skyhawk.

Heinemann initially tried to dissuade the resolute Captain Moorer from the suggestion. 'You'd ruin to good aircraft', Heinemann said. 'There just isn't enough space for the hoses, reels, drogues, and what-have-you.'

Heinemann knew that the current carrier-based heavy attack aircraft converted for aerial refuelling, the AJ Savage series, was nearing the end of its service life. He also knew the A4D's capabilities would be greatly expanded with added fuel. Thus, at the end of the long evening's discussion, he had some ideas in mind that would utilize the best suggestions both men made during the conversation.

Shortly thereafter, Heinemann developed plans for fitting both extra fuel tanks and refuelling gear in the bomb bay of the A3D. The much smaller size of the A4D, however, simply would never accommodate so much equipment. Hence, the Douglas team developed special 300—gallon (US) capacity streamlined refuelling tanks, subsequently called 'buddy stores', to be suspended from any of the three bomb rack hard points already built into the Skyhawk. With typical ingenuity, the new auxiliary fuel tanks were designed to be independent of the aircraft's power sources; an impeller in the nose of each tank provided power to drive the fuel pumps and operate the fuel line reel. With the centre-line-mounted buddy store in place, an A4D tanker could transfer to the receiving aircraft all of the host aircraft's external fuel, as well as half of its own internal capacity, for a total of 1,300 (US) gallons.

The inflight refuelling capability was standardised on the A4D–2, which was first flown on 26 March 1956 and delivered to the Fleet in 1957. A total of 542–2s were produced and, while they are easily recognisable by the long *straight* refuelling probe mounted on the lower

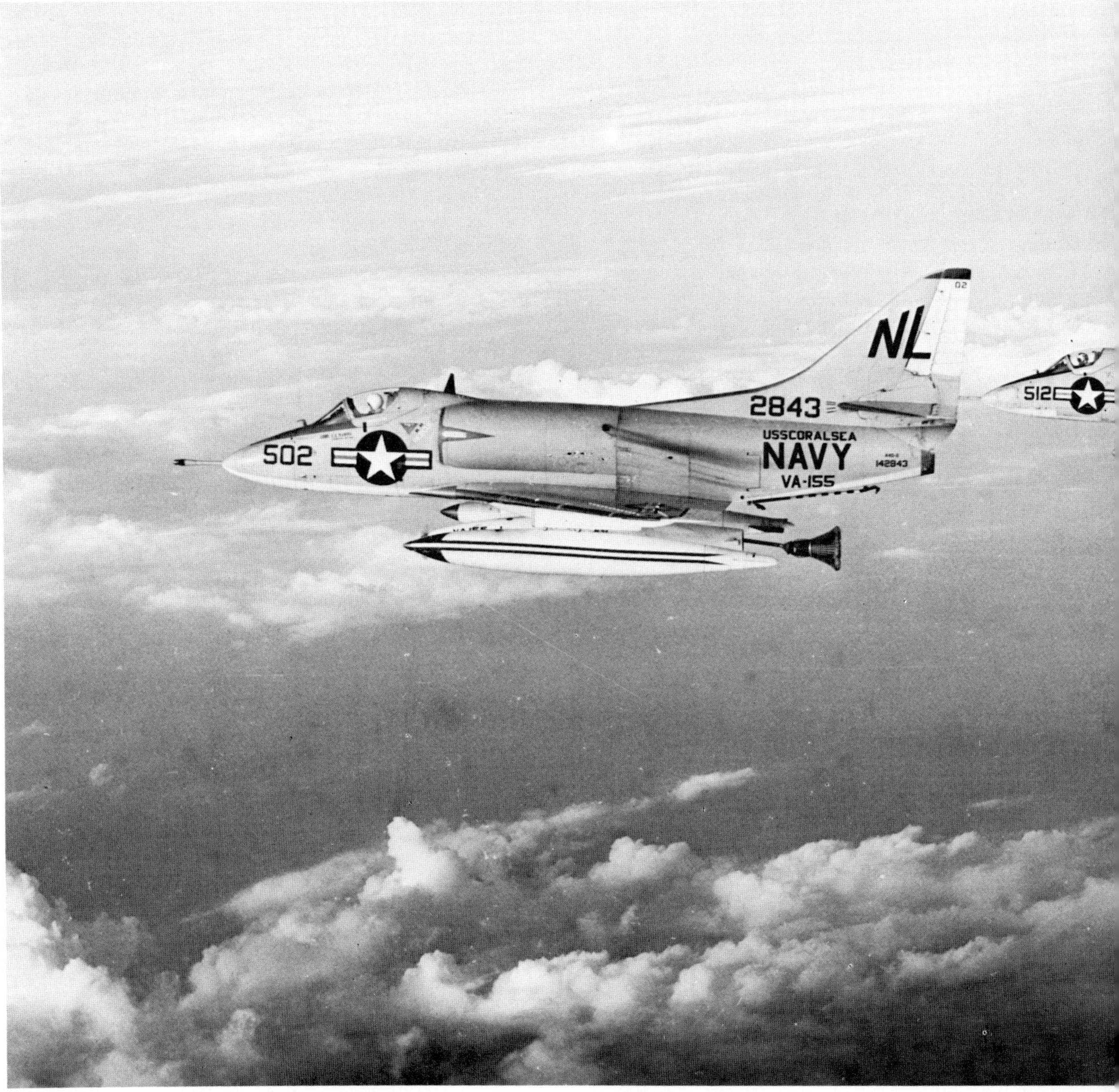
NL
2843
502
USSCORALSEA
NAVY
VA-155
142843
512

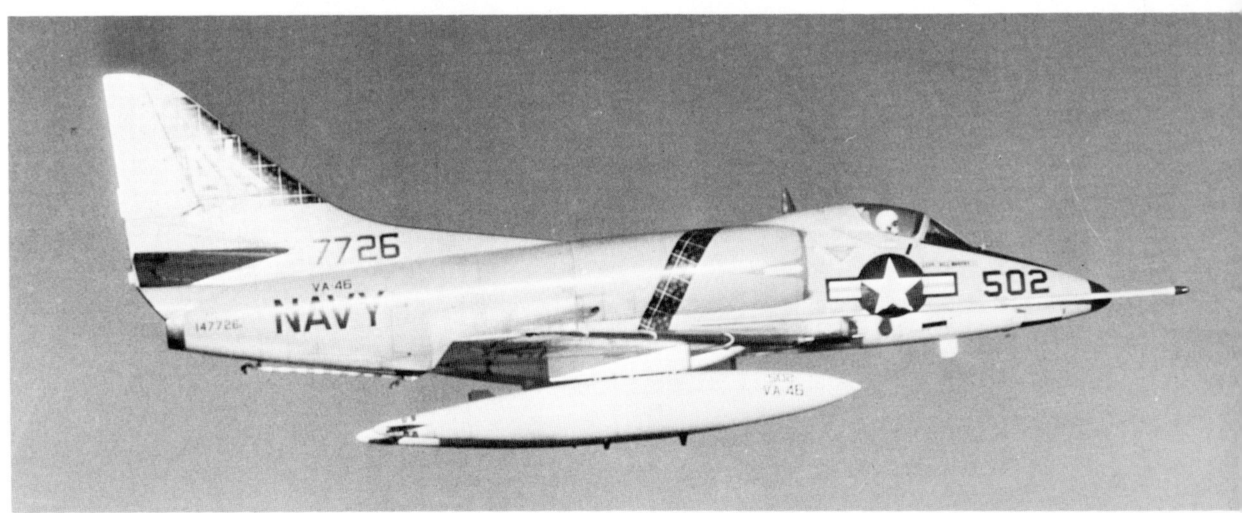

7726
VA 46
NAVY
147726
502

Two A4D-2 (A-4B) aircraft of the 'Silver Foxes' VA-155 with their refuelling drogues partially extended during the squadron's 1962 Western Pacific cruise aboard USS *Coral Sea* (CVA-43). The squadron's nickname comes from its commanding officer in 1958, Lieutenant Commander J. S. Smith, who was called the 'silver fox' by virtue of his silver-grey hair; the name soon stuck to the squadron

LEFT
A-4C of the 'Clansmen' VA-46 flown by Lieutenant Commander Bill Murphy during the squadron's 1962 deployment aboard USS *Shangri-La* (CVA-38). A year earlier, the 'Clansmen', so named because the first squadron commander was of Scottish descent, became the first jet attack squadron in the Fleet Air Jacksonville (Florida) area to fire live Bullpup air-to-surface guided missiles

starboard side of the forward fuselage, they included modification of 28 percent of the structure, including the 'tadpole' rudder, additional ordnance and navigation equipment and added control reliability. The structural improvements allowed the aircraft to clear 7*g* of stress. The A4D–2 was the first Skyhawk to carry the Bullpup air-to-surface missile.

The A4D–2 was initially equipped with the 7,700lb thrust Wright J65–W–16A engine, later uprated to the W–18 of 8,500lb thrust. It also introduced the dual hydraulic system that had originally been deleted as a weight-saving measure.

As the A4D series increased in Fleet service, weight became less of a consideration. The emphasis was on expanding operational capability. Hence, the next variant, the A4D–2N, added weight to gain the advantage of at least limited night-time and foul weather operational capability. Empty weight rose from 9,146 pounds for the A4D–2 to 9,728 pounds for the –2N, the primary difference being in additional avionics. The –2N was equipped with a small, simple APG–53A radar developed specifically for the Skyhawk, as well as a TPQ–10 blind bombing system, AJB–3 low-altitude bombing system and all-attitude reference, automatic flight control system (autopilot) and airstream direction detector.

The small, 16-inch-diameter, radar dish, still in use, performs mapping and ranging functions that enable the pilot to follow the terrain at relatively low altitude and high speed. Unlike other radar systems, however, it is *not* a weapons control system. The APG-53A radar equipment, housed in the nose cone, extended the A4D–2N's fuselage length to 40 feet $1\frac{1}{4}$ inches (against 39 feet $4\frac{3}{4}$ inches in the –2). The A4D–2N, most numerous of the Skyhawks, with 638 being produced, was first flown on 21 August 1958. It entered service with VMA–225 in March 1960 and VA–192 at the end of 1961.

There was to be an A4D-3 variant, powered by the 8,000lb-thrust Pratt & Whitney J52-P-2, but the order for 10 aircraft was subsequently cancelled. Also scrapped was the A4D-4, which would have been an A4D-2M with the J52 engine. However, it was quite clear that the time had come to replace the ageing single-shaft Wright J65 engine, which had passed its developmental peak, with an engine that offered more growth potential and the answer clearly lay in the two-spool Pratt & Whitney J52 series.

The 1,000th production Skyhawk, an A4D-2N, was delivered to the US Navy in February 1961. A few months later, on 12 July, the first A4D-5 made its appearance. Powered by the 8,500lb-thrust Pratt & Whitney J52-P-6, the -5 offered many clear improvements over its predecessors. The new lighter engine not only reduced empty weight to 9,284 lb, it also provided a slightly higher maximum speed (688 mph at sea level against 664 mph) and a 27-percent increase in range due to lower fuel consumption. An improved light-weight low-level ejection seat system was installed and two additional stores pylons were fitted to give the A4D-5 the most impressive punch of any Skyhawk yet to see service. Continued avionics improvements resulted in the -5 being equipped with Doppler radar, TACAN, radar altimeter and the new

A-4E of the 'Warhorses' VA-55 armed with Bullpup missiles during a practice flight in the United States. During the Vietnam War, the squadron used these air-to-surface missiles with a high degree of success

RIGHT
Buddy stores of the A-4C are seen in this view of a Skyhawk of the 'Bombing Broncos' VA-112. Also visible are the ejection chutes from where used shells from the aircraft's two 20-mm guns flow

AJB–3A LABS/all-attitude and heading reference. The first of the 498 A4D–5s entered service with VA–23 in November 1962 and became fully operational the following year.

While aircraft improvements were being developed, US Navy and Marine Corps units tested the new refinements under operational conditions. In early 1960, Commander J.K. Beling, commanding officer of VA–72, performed a record-setting over-water mission to test the 'buddy stores' inflight-refuelling equipment. He flew 2,250 miles non-stop from NAS Oceana in Virginia to a classified target area in the Caribbean and back in approximately $5\frac{1}{2}$ hours. Several hundred miles out to sea, the tanker aircraft refuelled Commander Beling's A4D, which then completed the mission alone, delivering a full-scale inert weapon successfully on target by loft bombing. It was the longest over-water A4D flight up to that time.

A short time later, during Exercise Blue Star on Taiwan, A4Ds of Marine Air Group 12 tested a new means to bring the Skyhawk closer to the ground units it would support in combat. Marine field engineers constructed a Short Expeditionary Landing Field (SELF) in which 9,852 aluminium planks were bolted together to form a 3,400-foot temporary runway. Colonel George C. Axtell, commanding officer of MAG–12, made the first landing, engaging MOREST (mobile arresting gear) designed to bring the aircraft to a halt within a relatively short distance. The Skyhawk normally required some 8,000 feet of reinforced concrete runway to make a landing. The combination of MOREST and aluminium planking more

NAVY
VA112

00

503

A4D-2 of VA-106 is moved forward to the port catapult of USS *Shangri-La* during a 1961 Caribbean exercise. The jet blast defector, at the rear of the aircraft, has already been raised to minimise the effect of engine exhaust on the A4Ds of VA-46 in the background

BELOW LEFT
A4D-2 (A-4B) assigned to the 'Gladiators' VA-106 is secured to the starboard catapult aboard USS *Shangri-La* (CVA-38) during the exercise Operation LANTFLEX 4-61 in the Caribbean Sea during June 1961. While the aircraft was flown by other pilots of VA-106, the markings indicate it was normally the personal aircraft of the commander of Carrier Air Group 10, Commander R. J. Stegg, whose name and title are stencilled on the fuselage side, below the cockpit. Traditionally, the air group commander's aircraft sports the 00 (so-called 'double nuts') identification numbers on the nose of the aircraft

BELOW CENTRE
A4D-2 of the 'Spirits' VA-76 approaching to land aboard USS *Intrepid* (CVA-11) in 1960

BELOW
A flight deck crewman aboard USS *Constellation* (CVA-64) signals Lieutenant B. V. Hagberg of the 'Roadrunners' VA-144 to add power to his A4D-2N to create proper tension on the catapult bridle prior to launching

nearly approximated the constraints that would exist in combat (and which, indeed, were used a few years later when the Marines set up an 'in-country' aviation facility at Chu Lai during the Vietnam War). The Marine A4Ds departed from the temporary airfield using JATO (Jet-Assisted Take-Off) bottles to take off from the short runway.

Also in 1960, Skyhawks went to war against the insect population of a nearby naval air station. A4Ds of VA-12 from NAS Cecil Field and VA-44 from NAS Jacksonville, Florida were fitted with insecticide canisters to spray an area near the Jacksonville air station. Pointing out the advantages of jet-propelled aircraft to spread insecticide against disease-carrying insects in an area that might be occupied by military personnel, entomoligist David Hayden said in *Naval Aviation News:* 'The average prop plane can move at 175 mph at the maximum and normally travels at a rate of 125 mph. With the jet we move at 500 mph, at an extremely low altitude of only 150 feet, capable of putting out 300 gallons a minute.'

The Multiple Carriage Bomb Racks, which became so important to Skyhawk missions in the Vietnam War and other events, were developed by a Navy officer and two Marine Corps officers assigned to air development squadron VX-5 at the Naval Air Facility at China Lake, California. Commander Dale Cox, Marine Major K.P. Rice and Marine Captain H.W. Fitch conceived and designed the MCBRs, which allow six 250lb bombs to be carried on each of the two wing stations and six 500lb bombs on the centre line station. Prior to take-off the pilot selects whether to release the bombs from a rack singly or in a salvo. Following evaluation by the Naval Ordnance Test Centre (NOTC) at China Lake and the NATC at Patuxent River, VMA-225 at MCAS Cherry Point, North Carolina, conducted final operational tests. The

Instrument panel of an A4D-2 (A-4B) Skyhawk shows the compactness of the various controls. Improvements in the instrument cluster in later models added to the aircraft's effectiveness

RIGHT
Commander R. C. Fowler, Jr., Commander of Carrier Air Group 1, just beginning his quick run down the port catapult of USS *Franklin D. Roosevelt* (CVA-42) during 1963 deployment with the Sixth Fleet in the Mediterranean. When not used by the Air Group Commander, this A-4C was operated by the 'Flying Ubangis' VA-12. In background are Vought F-8E Crusaders of the 'Red Rippers' VF-11

ABOVE RIGHT
Before the steam of the previous cat shot (catapult launch) clears, an A-4B of Marine attack squadron VMA-324 is taxied onto the port catapult of USS *Independence* (CVA-62) during the carrier's 1963 cruise in the Mediterranean

BELOW RIGHT
A4D-2N (A-4C) of the 'Blue Hawks' VA-72 comes to the end of its arrested landing aboard USS *Independence* (CVA-62) during 1961 Mediterranean deployment. The flight deck crewman chasing after the aircraft will disengage the aircraft's tailhook from the arrestor wire

AG
8485
NAVY
305
305

multiple bomb racks were subsequently manufactured by Douglas and supplied to the appropriate squadrons.

The Skyhawk's ordnance delivery capability was enhanced further with development of the Martin Bullpup-A air-to-surface missile, a liquid-fuelled rocket weapon of considerable accuracy. When VA-46 became the first Bullpup-equipped jet attack squadron in the Fleet Air Jacksonville area, in November 1960, seven A4D-2N pilots fired live Bullpup missiles. Best score was achieved by the squadron safety officer, Lieutenant W.H. Byng, who recorded an average error-from-target of 11·57 feet.

Early in their operational career A4Ds were deployed exclusively aboard attack aircraft carriers (CVAs). With the designation of anti-submarine warfare carriers (CVSs) beginning in 1957, however, naval planners were looking long range at providing tactical support for the ASW air groups aboard the CVSs. The CVSs were all CVAs of the *Essex* class, which had already demonstrated the capability of supporting Skyhawks, so the 'trial marriage' of the A4D and the CVS was a natural development. Indeed, the first ASW carrier to deploy Skyhawks was USS *Essex* (CVS-9), which had already been host to A4D squadrons prior to her 8 March 1960 redesignation as a CVS. During a 19-day deployment in 1961, *Essex's* ASW air group CVSG-60 of Grumman S2F Trackers (VS-34 and VS-39), Douglas AD-5W Skyraiders (VAW-12 Det 45) and Sikorsky HSS-1 Seabat helicopters (HS-9) was joined by 12 A4D-2Ns of VA-34 from NAS Cecil Field, Florida. During the deployment, VA-34 proved their tactical value to the ASW air group in a round of flying that totalled 768 flight hours and included 512 'traps' (arrested landings aboard the carrier).

On 18 September 1962, all American armed services adopted a new method of aircraft designation. The US Secretary of Defence, Robert S. McNamara, used this as one of several devices to achieve a measure of standardisation among the armed forces. Hence, the distinctive Navy system of mission-manufacturer-number gave way to designations similar to those long in use by the US Air Force. Under the new system the AD Skyraider series became the A-1, the AJ Savage series the A-2, the A3D Skywarrior the A-3, the A4D Skyhawk series the A-4, the A3J Vigilante the A-5 and Grumman's new A2F Intruder the A-6. Any sub-series of the main classification was denoted by a letter in alphabetical order, including accommodations for *most* omissions. In the case of the Skyhawk series, the relation of the old classifications to the new was:

Old	New	Old	New
A4D-1	A-4A	A4D-3	(not produced)
A4D-2	A-4B	A4D-4	(not produced)
A4D-2N	A-4C	A4D-5	A-4E

Superstition? During VA-55's 13th cruise to the Western Pacific, in 1963, this A-4C (BuNo 148488) had to make a wheels-up landing at a shore base. The combination of flame-retarding foam laid on the runway, field arresting gear and the pilot's skill in bringing the Skyhawk in on its auxiliary fuel tanks, combined to result in no great damage to the aircraft

ABOVE LEFT
A-4E Skyhawk of the 'Warhorses' VA-55 deployed aboard USS *Ticonderoga* (CVA-14) refuels a de Havilland Sea Vixen FAW.1, from HMS *Victorious* during joint operations in June 1964. Two months later, the 'Warhorses' were involved in the Tonkin Gulf incident that triggered the American commitment to the Vietnam War

RIGHT
A-4E of the 'Hornets' VA-44 shows the thermal shield in the fully closed position. The device was to be used when delivering nuclear weapons so that, after detonation, the pilot would be protected against the nuclear flash

VMA-225 made both Marine Corps and Skyhawk history during a trans-Atlantic flight that began on 8 October 1962. It was the first time a Marine Corps attack squadron had ever made the trans-Atlantic trip and certainly marked the longest A-4 hop up to that time. 16 A-4s left MCAS Cherry Point for Kindley Air Force Base, Bermuda, where they refuelled before setting out on the nearly 3,000-mile course to the US Naval Station at Rota, Spain. Mechanical difficulties forced one A-4C to return to Kindley AFB, but the others proceeded to NS Rota, being refuelled twice *en route* by Lockheed KC-130F Hercules tanker aircraft from Marine aerial refueller/transporter squadron VMGR-252. The flight, led by Lieutenant Colonel Edwin A. Harper, commanding officer, arrived in Spain the following day. Accompanied by Colonel Jack E. Conger, commander of MAG-14, the flight returned to Cherry point via a seven-hour non-stop flight from Lajes Field in the Azores to Kindley AFB and an overnight stay in Bermuda. Following their 16 October departure from Lajes, the 15 A-4s again logged two in-flight refuellings from VMGR-252 tankers.

The importance of long hops in A-4 aircraft was reinforced on 19 June 1963, when two made a non-stop trans-continental flight. Lieutenant Commander Dave Leue and Lieutenant Jerry Tappan of VA-81, the first Atlantic Fleet operational unit to receive the A-4E with the more fuel-efficient J52 engine, departed NAS

TOP
A4D-5 (A-4E) of the Naval Ordnance Test Centre carrying both Mk. 81 bombs and Bullpup air-to-surface missiles

ABOVE
A4D-5 (A-4E) of the Naval Ordnance Test Centre at China Lake, California with clusters of inert Mk. 81 bombs during development of multiple carriage bomb racks

RIGHT
A4D-2N (A-4C) of the 'Vampires' VX-5 air development squadron, testing the multiple-carriage bomb racks (MCBRs) developed by the squadron

NAVY

Lemoore, California, at 0927 hours and landed at NAS Oceana, Virginia, four hours and 19 minutes later. The two pilots flew their A–4Es a distance of 2,100 nautical miles without assistance. Previously, A–4s had required in-flight refuelling to cover a similar distance.

A two-place trainer version was ordered into production in 1964 by revising the A–4E contract to specify that the last two aircraft in the production run were to be altered to include the features required for training purposes. The changes included a 28-inch fuselage extension to accommodate the second seat and the necessary dual controls and instruments, as well as a new Douglas-designed Escapac IC–3 'zero-zero' ejection seat, which allowed safe egress from a disabled aircraft at ground level and zero forward speed. Also added were nose-wheel steering and lift spoilers to facilitate crosswind landings. These features were developed simultaneously for the A–4F and this quickly led to the redesignation of the two-seat variant.

The first flight of the TA–4E took place on 30 June 1965 at Palmdale, California. The aircraft was powered by the Pratt & Whitney J52–P–8A of 9,300lb thrust, a further improvement over the 8,500lb thrust J52–P–6A used in the standard A–4E. In production, the aircraft was designated TA–4F, beginning a long and successful use of the two-seat Skyhawk that continues to this day.

The TA–4F retained most of the armament capability of the single-place A–4. However, most of the 241 TA–4Fs were subsequently converted to TA–4J specification, adding to the 292 TA–4Js (including 17 for Israel) built entirely as that variant. Since the TA-4J is intended solely as an advanced trainer for the Navy Training Command, some of the ordnance systems are deleted and the less-powerful Pratt & Whitney J52–P–6 engine has been installed.

During the Vietnam War, the A–4 was a prime US Navy and Marine Corps attack aircraft and to replace Skyhawks lost in action the A–4F was ordered in 1965. It was similar to the A–4E except in that it incorporated the nosewheel steering, lift spoilers, Escapac IC–3 ejection seat and uprated J52–P–8A engine introduced in the TA–4F. The A–4F first flew on 31 August 1966.

A further improvement added later was a large dorsal fairing, aft of the cockpit, to accommodate additional special electronic gear necessitated by the special conditions of the Vietnam War. Kits were supplied for aircraft already delivered to the Fleet and those aircraft not yet delivered were so modified at the Douglas plant. The avionics pod was fitted on all existing operational A–4Es and some A–4Cs and 100 A–4Fs were re-equipped with the more powerful J52–P–401 engine, which required slightly larger air intakes.

Rear Admiral Robert E. Kirksey had a variety of Skyhawk experiences. As did so many A–4 pilots, he converted from fighter aircraft (FJ–3s) to an early A–4 variant. In his case, this was in 1962, when he was assigned to VA–125, the Readiness Training Squadron (RTS) which qualified Skyhawk pilots for the Pacific Fleet. He subsequently flew with VA–195 before becoming executive officer and commanding officer of VA–55.

At-sea testing of MCBRs was carried out by the Naval Air Test Centre, based at NAS Patuxent River, Maryland. In this view, Y/A4D-2 BuNo 142089 (early series A-4B devoted to testing) is prepared for catapult launch from an *Essex*-class carrier. For this test, MCBRs are loaded with six 500-lb. and twelve 250-lb. bombs

Technicians attach a High Performance Gun (Hipeg), externally-mounted 20-mm cannon pod, to an A4D. Augmenting the regular 20-mm cannon, seen above in the wing root, the Hipeg fires ammunition at the rate of 4,000 rounds per minute on pin-point targets. A one-second burst can deliver on a tank target the equivalent of a 4,000-lb load dropped from 1,000 feet – with, of course, much greater accuracy

LEFT
Exposed view of the Hipeg 20-mm cannon. Hard-hitting, fast-firing and highly accurate, the Hipeg works on the revolver principle. A large single cylinder feeds two barrels, each firing at 66 rounds per second

During several tours, Kirksey flew the A-4C, A-4E and A-4F and noted successive improvements in each one. He also had some harrowing operational experiences which, when subsequently shared with American naval aviation safety officials, added to the body of knowledge needed to make further improvements in the aircraft.

In one instance, a night-time catapult launch from USS *Constellation* (CVA-64), nearly ended in tragedy, when the APG-53 radar screen assembly flew back and lodged against the control column. Admiral Kirksey recalls:

'When you take a catapult shot, you become airborne in two seconds. In that time a lot of things would "want" to come back into your lap. In one case, an expansion band that should have held the radar unit failed and a set of screws to do the same task were either too short or stripped. Consequently, as I was catapulted, the whole APG-53 "box" came out of the console and pushed right up against the stick.

Although the radar unit has outside dimensions of about 5 inches by 5 inches, about the size of a small television set, it is about 18 inches deep. So, if it flies out, as it did on this occasion, it takes up practically all the free space inside the small cockpit. It winds up almost in your lap, lodged between you and the edge of the console.

'That's what happened to me; but, as it came out, I managed to pull the stick all the way back and to the left, and I was stuck in that position – taking off with a full load of six Mk 82, 500-pound bombs. The aircraft went nose-high and then into a left roll. At about 70 or 80 degress into the roll I knew I wasn't going to get out of the airplane. If I ejected at that point, I knew I'd go straight down into the water.

'I let it continue to roll and, as I couldn't reach up over my head to activate the regular ejection system, I reached down for an alternate ejection system, placed at the bottom of the seat. I planned to "punch out" at the level point in the roll. As I reached down, however, the act of sliding my arm down along the side took the pressure off the corner of the radar unit and it just dropped into my lap.

'Now I was easily able to straighten out the aircraft, but I had another problem, as I had already started the ejection sequence. When you pull the alternate ejection handle about an inch and a half, it fires – and I had pulled it about an inch when the APG-53 suddenly fell out. I immediately stopped everything and waited. But nothing happened. The ejection seat didn't fire and the radar unit was still in my lap.

'While all this was going on, I was losing altitude and, by this time, was almost on the water. Once I recovered, I climbed to 10,000 feet and began to orbit the carrier. I didn't know whether the ejection seat would fire when I made contact with the flight deck, but I did want to get back to the ship, so I radioed to our people and had them check the flight manuals. Meanwhile, I dumped some of my fuel to lighten my load.

'A check of the flight manuals indicated that, to the best of everyone's knowledge, the seat probably would not fire due to the impact of landing on the carrier deck. That wasn't much of a guarantee, but I decided to take a chance.

'After the rest of the launch had gotten off, I came back

The A4D Skyhawk could carry three Hipeg gun pods under the wings and fuselage to deliver a very hard punch to ground targets. Alternating tracer rounds show the effect of the pilot's aim. Note the discarded shell casings streaming from the pods

CHINA
LAKE
5063
NAVY

NAVAL
MISSILE
CENTER
073
5073
RESCUE
NO SMOKING
TRAINER
Thiokol
CHEMICAL CORPORATION

ABOVE
Among the weapons available to the Skyhawk is the Mk. 56 air-launched mine, seen here attached to the centre-line mounting of an A-4B

LEFT
A-4B of the Naval Missile Center at Point Mugu, California about to be loaded with a ATM-12B Bullpup training missile

to the carrier. The landing was uneventful and, indeed, the ejection seat did *not* fire. I had managed to put the APG–53 unit back into the console, and since everything "wants" to move *forward* on landing, I had no further trouble with the radar popping out.

'Everything went smoothly until the Air Boss, who runs the flight deck from a position up in the "island" superstructure, told me to taxi to Number 2 aircraft elevator. Once I was on the elevator, however, they started to lower it to the hangar deck. When I asked what was going on, I was told they were going to take me into the hangar bay to dis-arm the ejection seat.

'I quickly put a stop to that. I radioed back: "If this seat goes, I don't want to become part of the hangar bay. I'd much rather take my chances getting airborne as far as the seat will take me and come down over the water."

'The seat was dis-armed on the flight deck and it turned out that the activating mechanism was within a quarter of an inch of hitting the firing position. As a result of that incident, the squadron made its own "fix" to ensure that the APG–53 unit didn't come out of the console again. Some of our people fitted each of our aircraft with two straps across the unit, on the console, as an added means of keeping the unit in place during the rapid acceleration of the catapult stroke. Douglas Aircraft subsequently made a

A4D-2 of the 'Fighting Redcocks' VA-22 tips on to its starboard wing just after landing aboard USS *Midway* (CVA-41) during 1960 Western Pacific deployment

The A4D-2 comes to rest on the starboard wingtip after nosewheel movement caused it to veer off course on landing

142889
NAVY
VA-22

Lieutenant (junior grade) Bill Belden of the 'Wild Aces' VA-152 made a normal landing aboard USS *Shangri-La* (CVA-38) during flight operations in July 1970. After the tailhook was disengaged, Belden added power to taxi. On braking, however, his right brake failed and the A-4E veered to the left. Here, Chief Aviation Boatswain's Mate Joe Hammond pushes on the starboard wingtip in hopes of turning the aircraft

RIGHT
Despite Hammond's efforts, the Skyhawk went off the flight deck and into the port-side catwalk. Fearing the aircraft would continue into the water, the pilot ejected. Chief Hammond was subsequently knocked over by debris from the ejection sequence

permanent fix on the unit and that was applied to aircraft throughout the Fleet.'

Although Admiral Kirksey never had to use the ejection seat to make an emergency escape from the aircraft, he vividly recalls another close encounter under less than ideal circumstances:

'When we were back ashore, we had a procedure of refuelling the aircraft after completing night-time Field Carrier Landing Practice (FCLP). After the last practice hop, we would taxi into the fuel pit, where ground-crewmen would "hot" refuel the aircraft so it would be all set for the next morning's flights.

'While I was waiting to get into the fuel pits after my last FCLP, I went through our standard routine of returning all the switches to the right position and "bottoming" the seat so it was in the lowest position and could be adjusted as necessary by the next person to fly the aircraft; I usually flew with the seat high, so lowering it was a courtesy to some taller person who might fly that aircraft the next day.

In fact, we levied fines against pilots who failed to leave the aircraft in the right condition for the next person – and, as the squadron skipper, I certainly had to follow that rule strictly.

'I was in the process of lowering the seat when it suddenly felt as if I were being ejected. We later learned that someone had dropped a pencil down the rail on which the seat is raised or lowered and that pencil got jammed in such a way as to activate part of the ejection sequence.

'Normally, you begin the sequence in an A–4 by pulling the face curtain down from the top of the seat. As the seat goes up the rail, a small sear is knocked off to trigger bladders on the back of the seat that subsequently separate the pilot from the seat. Two big, carbon dioxide-activated bladders actually "kick" the pilot about 10 feet away from the seat. Then the parachute deploys to carry him safely down to ground level.

'As I was lowering the seat, the pencil jammed and broke the sear, which automatically activated the bladders. They pushed me all the way up against the top of the cockpit, as far forward as I could go. In that position, my feet were now off the brakes and, with the engine still running, the aircraft began to roll forward.

'I could still touch the "mike" button on the throttle, but I couldn't do anything else with the throttle. So I hit the mike and announced that I had a problem and hoped the control tower could get someone to help me. Just then, two young groundcrewmen, who must have been tremendous runners, could tell something was wrong. They each grabbed a chock and took off after me on foot. They caught up with the airplane, and threw their chocks down in front of the wheels and brought the plane to a halt.

'Once the aircraft was stopped, then the groundcrewmen began working to get me out of it. But it occurred to me that, once they raised the canopy, the force of the bladders might push me right out of the cockpit, head first. So, while they worked on the canopy, I managed to reach my survival knife and began jabbing at the main bladder,

While Belden was being rescued, the flight deck crew quickly acted to save the aircraft. A tie-down chain was applied to the A-4E's tailhook to stop the aircraft from going over the side. Firefighters were also on hand, but not needed. The aircraft was pulled back onto the flight deck, repaired and later returned to duty

U.S. NAVY

NM
AVY
502
408
NM
150327

to puncture it and relieve the pressure.

'After that, we had the squadron's metalsmiths make a small puncturing tool that all of the pilots could use if they got into a similar situation. Eventually, all A–4s came through with a sharp puncturing tool mounted up on the windscreen. It is in a small insert, so as to not be hazardous in itself, but to be available to a pilot who might inadvertently activate the ejection seat bladders.'

On 28 April 1967 the Douglas Aircraft Company and the McDonnell Aircraft Company merged to form the McDonnell Douglas Corporation. That development occurred just as production of the Navy's last single-seat Skyhawk, the A–4F, was winding down, but it certainly did not presage the end of the A–4 line.

Indeed, since there are generally several variants of a matured design in service at any one time, improvements made to later models are usually incorporated into earlier versions. The modification is done either by the manufacturer or by the service's dedicated rework facility.

A-4C of US Marine Corps attack squadron VMA-223's Detachment T makes a barrier landing aboard USS *Yorktown* (CVS-10) in 1964. The aircraft lost its tailhook in a previous landing attempt. At this time, attack aircraft were not normally assigned to anti-submarine warfare aircraft carriers, such as USS *Yorktown*, but small detachments were assigned to various larger units. In this case, the aircraft is from a detachment assigned to ASW air group CVSG-55

LEFT
A-4C of the 'Dambusters' VA-195 slides to a halt on the flight deck of USS *Bon Homme Richard* (CVA-31) after engaging the barrier during flight operations in 1965. An inoperable nose wheel was the cause. The use of the barrier enables Navy pilots to land on the ship in a damaged aircraft, which, later, can often be salvaged

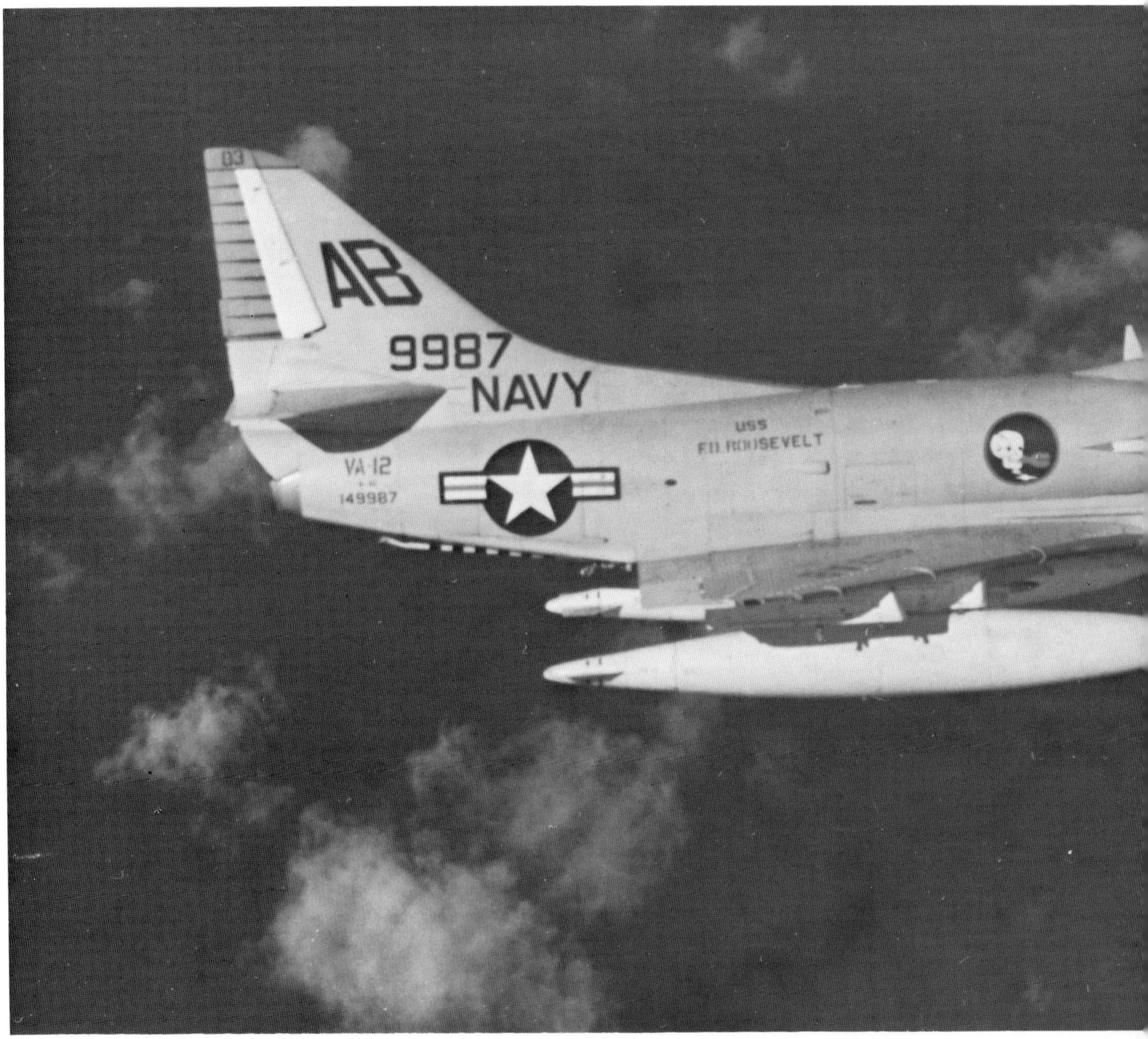
03
AB
9987
NAVY
USS
VA-12
149987

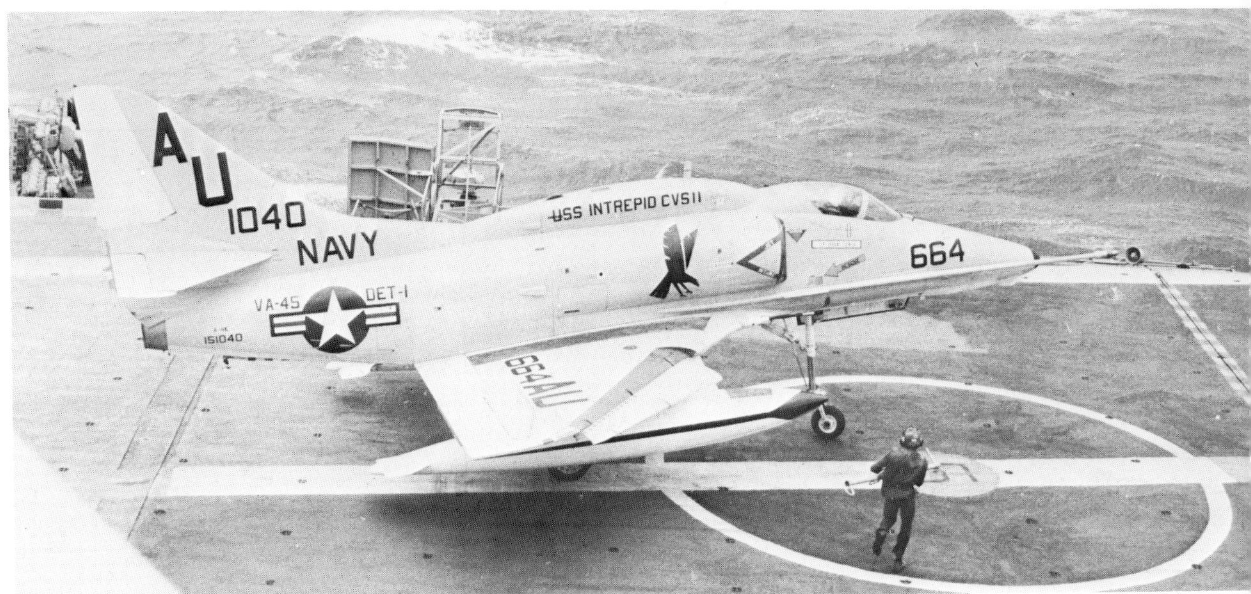

AU
1040
NAVY
USS INTREPID CVS11
664
VA-45
DET-1
151040
664AU

A-4C of the 'Flying Ubangis' VA-12 during 1963 deployment aboard USS *Franklin D. Roosevelt* (CVA-42). The squadron insignia, on the fuselage side, shows the kiss of death that led to the unit's unusual nickname

BELOW LEFT
In the early 1970s, as the US Navy consolidated its aircraft carrier force CVAs and CVSs under the CV concept, tactical aircraft were deployed aboard CVSs and ASW aircraft became part of CVA air groups. Shown here aboard USS *Intrepid* (CVS-11) in 1973, is an A-4E of Detachment 1 of the 'Blackbirds' VA-45 taxying up to the catapult

BELOW
Carrying a Dart gunnery target package, an A-4E of the 'Unique Antiques' VC-1 flies off the coast of Hawaii. Composite squadrons such as VC-1 routinely operate a variety of aircraft to help Fleet surface and air units accomplish a number of training objectives. Originally commissioned as fleet utility squadron VJ-1 on 5 October 1925, VC-1 is the US Navy's oldest composite squadron and is a longtime user of the A-4 series

A-4E (BuNo 149652) assigned to the Naval Air Test Center (NATC) at NAS Patuxent River, Maryland, flies over that facility while evaluating in-flight refuelling equipment

NAVY

TA-4F (BuNo 152848) was test flown by a NATC crew without the canopy on 6 May 1966 during stall tests. Maximum drag has already been induced by lowering the undercarriage and extending the dive brakes

In some cases, a considerable number of a certain model may be reworked to the point where they merit a different designation. Thus, when 100 A–4C aircraft were updated to A–4F standards in terms of equipment and control systems, including the distinctive avionics pod on top of the fuselage, they were re-classified as the A–4L (they retained the old J65 engines and were, therefore, not completely up to A–4F standards). This programme was undertaken at Naval Air Rework Facilities (NARF), with the first flight of the A–4L type taking place on 21 August 1969. The A–4Ls were assigned to Navy and Marine Corps air reserve units, where they served until they were replaced by early model Ling-Temco-Vought A–7A Corsair II aircraft in the mid 1970s.

On 17 May 1963, the Navy had announced a design competition for a new light attack aircraft (VAL) to replace

the A–4s in both Navy and Marine Corps squadrons. The A–7A Corsair II was named the winner of the VAL competition almost a year later and the Navy eventually phased out the single-seat A–4 in favour of this new aircraft.

Despite its improved performance, however, the A–7A presented some distinct disadvantages for the Marine Corps. It soon became clear that the A–7 series would cost far more to maintain than the smaller, less complex A–4. Moreover, the A–7 had mission capabilities well in excess of those required by the Marines for relatively short-range close air support missions.

With the availability of the more powerful Pratt & Whitney J52–P–408A engine, with a 20 percent increase in thrust and no significant rise in fuel consumption, the Marines ordered into production the A–4M model, a vastly improved version of the Skyhawk for their tactical operations. The added power greatly enhanced the Marines' short-field capability, for the first time making possible A-4 operations from 4,000-foot runways.

The new engine, which developed 11,200lb thrust, allowed an increase in manoeuvrability, rate of climb and acceleration, thereby enhancing the aircraft's combat survival chances. Speed of the A–4M is in the high subsonic range, approximately 700mph.

Other A–4M changes included a greater ammunition capacity for internally mounted 20mm or 30mm guns, a more powerful generator, a self-contained engine starter and a larger windscreen and pilot canopy, providing greater headroom and visibility.

The A–4M made its maiden flight on 10 April 1970 and deliveries began a year later, with VMA–324 at MCAS

NAVY
DANGER
RESCUE
A-4E
150050

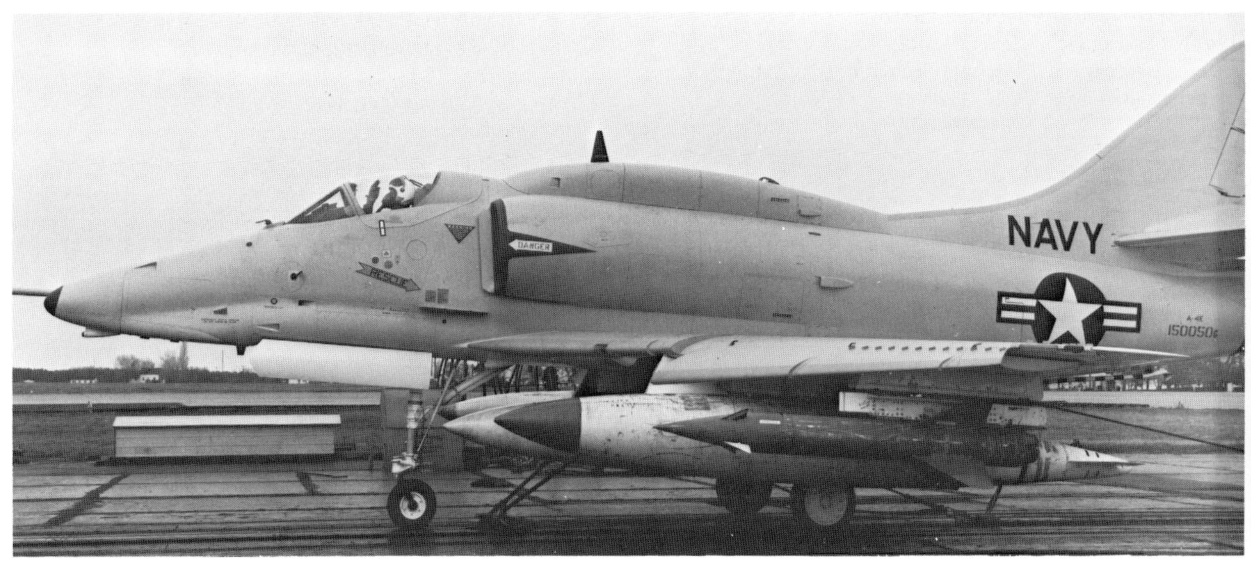

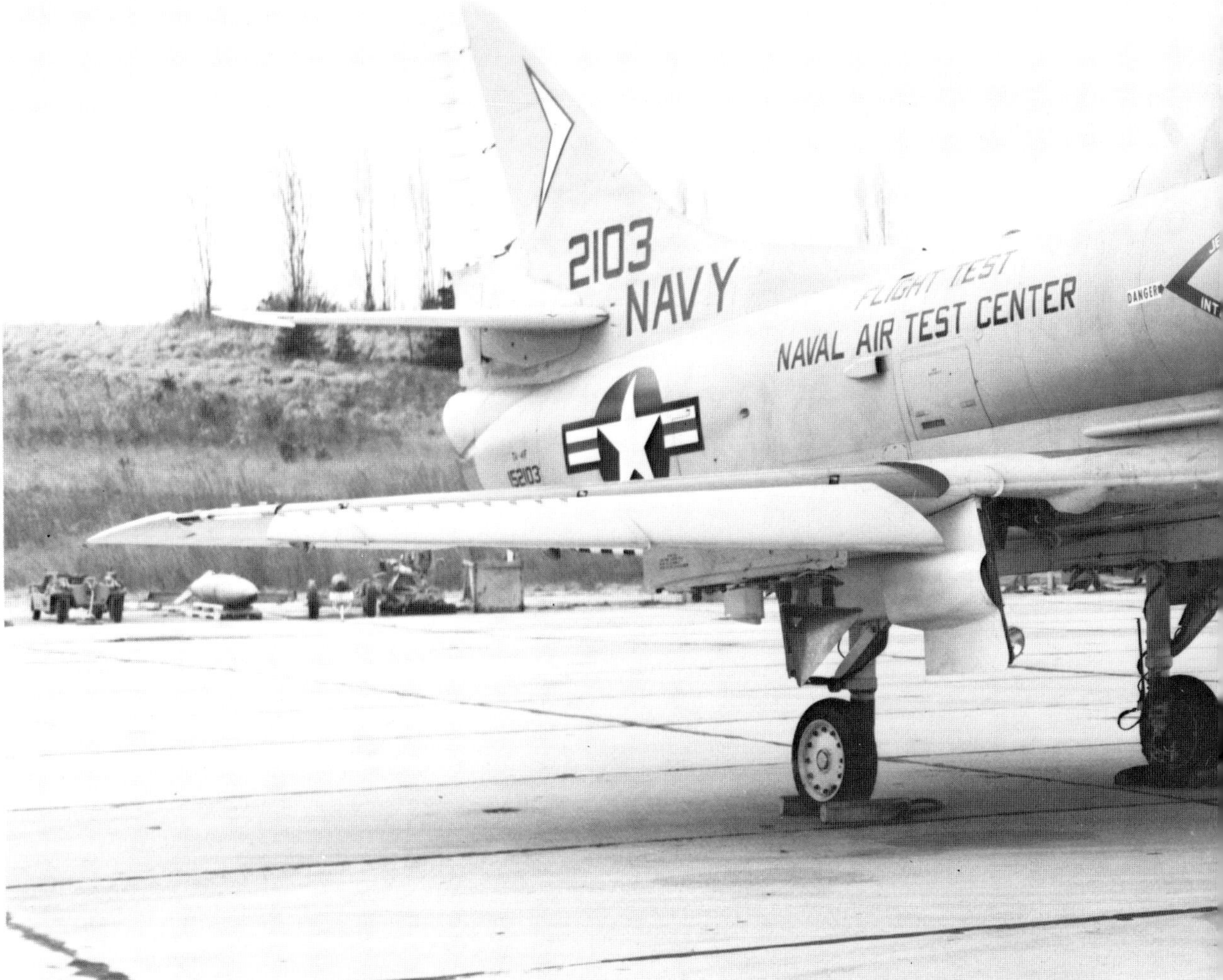
2103
NAVY
FLIGHT TEST
NAVAL AIR TEST CENTER
DANGER

A-4E (BuNo 150050) was catapult tested at NATC on 13 March 1967 with various simulated fuel and armaments load. For such tests, ordnance was not live, but filled with water to attain proper weight

The second pre-production TA-4F (BuNo 152103) and its sister aircraft, (BuNo 152102) were used for several years by NATC crews to evaluate various refinements to the two-seat Skyhawk

Beaufort, South Carolina being the first operational squadron. McDonnell Douglas built a total of 158 A–4Ms and converted two A–4Fs to the same standards.

The last Skyhawk delivered – the 2,960th aircraft in the series – was an A–4M, which went to VMA–331 at MCAS Cherry Point on 27 February 1979. The distinctive angular rudder fin has since been seen on more than the A–4Ms produced for the US Marine Corps. The last variant of Skyhawk offered many features that appealed to the Israelis, who ordered a type know as the A–4N for their use.

The McDonnell Douglas A–4 Skyhawk, series has clearly proven itself to be one of the dominant combat aircraft of the post-Korean War period and much of that proof came during America's long and intensive involvement in the Vietnam War.

4

Vietnam: The Crucible

The Skyhawk had been ready for operations during the Lebanon Crisis of 1958 and in subsequent incidents of international unrest, but its first extensive test as a modern combat aircraft did not come until the United States broadened its involvement in the Vietnam War of 1964-73.

While the military objective of US operation in Vietnam was to stabilize the government of South Vietnam, political constraints imposed by Washington often impeded the achievement of that objective. Successive administrations placed numerous restrictions on targets, methods of attack and types and quantities of weapons used – all in an unsuccessful attempt to keep the Soviet Union or the People's Republic of China from assuming active roles in the war. Thus, throughout the course of the war, while Soviet and Chinese advisors directly assisted their North Vietnamese allies and vast quantities of their aid kept North Vietnam viable, ever greater daring and skill were required of the American combatants on their missions. A–4 pilots, for example, were required to operate with surgeon-like precision to deliver their ordnance on targets without violating the numerous pre-conditions placed on them by government strategists half a world away.

The A–4's unique qualifications for the intense combat environment of south-east Asia are recalled by Rear Admiral Robert E. Kirksey, who flew over 200 combat missions from the flight decks of three different aircraft carriers during some of the heaviest fighting of the war:

'The small physical size of the aircraft brought with it an interesting psychological factor. You felt almost as if you were indestructible, since your aircraft was so small to hit. There are no statistics to support the conclusion that we were any less vulnerable in the A–4, but we sure had a feeling of security. We would talk to F–4 Phantom or A–5

Two A-4Cs of the 'Silver Foxes' VA-155 from USS *Coral Sea* (CVA-43) proceed over North Vietnam to targets carrying four 1,000-lb bombs

Vigilante pilots – both types flew – pretty high-density airplanes – and we would tell them we couldn't understand why they wanted to fly around in such big airplanes when there were these nice, safe little "scooters".

'From a very practical standpoint, the small size of the A–4 meant you could take several holes through the airplane and often continue to fly without even knowing you were hit – until you got back aboard the carrier and someone found the holes. In other aircraft, such as the F–4 with its two side-by-side engines in a very dense airframe, sometimes a few holes in the airplane would result in the loss of your hydraulic systems. In many cases, that meant having to eject from the airplane.

'I felt the A–4 was a very survivable (*sic*) airplane. It was small enough so that it wasn't like an aluminium cloud, flying around for anyone to take a pot-shot at. Although we were often heavily laden with bombs and only doing about 330 knots, by the time ground forces knew they should be looking for something to shoot at, we had already moved on.

'The A–4 cockpit was arranged so that you could devote a lot of time to the outside environment. This is absolutely essential to the successful completion of combat missions. After having developed a basic familiarity with the airplane, you could drop your left hand in the cockpit and be right at the throttle and speedbrakes. The handle to the control stick, with all ordanance dropping systems and guns and rocket-firing trigger, was very convenient. The armament panel was easy to set up and we usually armed a lot of our stations prior to rolling in on the target. That way, during the heaviest flak, all you had to do was hit one switch and you were ready to do your mission. In short, the "switchology" of the A–4 was so simple, that at the most crucial times when you needed to be able to concentrate on the outside environment, you were able to do so.

'I got to the point where, at times, it seemed my head was on a swivel. This was especially true when we were operating around Hanoi, where there was a lot of surface-to-air missile (SAM) activity. But, while I was busy looking over the target area, it was quite simple just to

drop my arm down to the master arming switch, feel it and know I had the station switches on. In the same area, right on the throttle quadrant, we had the ability to jettison "chaff" to confuse enemy radar, and also to energise an on-board camera to record the results of a run in on the target. In all respects, the A–4 was an efficient fighting machine.'

American involvement in Vietnam followed closely the disastrous French attempt to defeat Viet Minh forces opposed to the former colonial power. The dissolution of the French colonial holdings in Indo-China in 1954 resulted in the partitioning of Vietnam, with the territorial integrity of the two states presumably guaranteed by the signatories of the Geneva Conference of Vietnam. However, the non-communist government in South Vietnam was constantly threatened by Viet Cong guerrillas trained and supplied by communist North Vietnam. The Saigon government requested aid from the United States and America's contribution to the stability of South Vietnam, in terms of air power and advisors, steadily grew.

Matters reached a critical state on 2 August 1964, however, when elements of the US Navy's Task Force (TF) 77 were attacked in international waters by Soviet-built P–4 class torpedo boats flying the colours of North Vietnam. Two of the three boats fired torpedos at the destroyer USS *Maddox* (DD–731) and exchanged fire with the American vessel. The fast-moving attackers were driven off by fierce fire from the US destroyer and, subsequently, sustained further damage from four Vought F–8E Crusader jet fighters launched from the

Douglas A-4C Skyhawks of the 'Stingers' VA-113 vent excess fuel prior to coming aboard the nuclear-powered aircraft carrier USS *Enterprise* (CVAN-65) cruising in the Tonkin Gulf during combat operations off North Vietnam in 1967. During that deployment, VA-113 Skyhawks flew some 2,287 combat sorties and delivered over 4.9 million pounds of ordnance, flying both day and night missions

aircraft carrier USS *Ticonderoga* (CVA–14). At least two of the torpedo boats were sunk.

This unprovoked attack on the high seas was followed by another attack two days later. Reinforcing the American right to patrol international waters, a strengthened TF 77 patrol returned to the Gulf of Tonkin. The *Maddox* was accompanied by the destroyer USS *Turner Joy* (DD–951) and the World War II-vintage *Ticonderoga* was joined by the newer and larger super-carrier USS *Constellation* (CVA–64). All ships and aircraft were under strict orders to fire only if fired upon. Thus, when North Vietnamese torpedo boats initiated an attack on the night of 4/5 August, the American response was swift and sure – and marked the A–4's first combat foray in the long and costly Vietnam War.

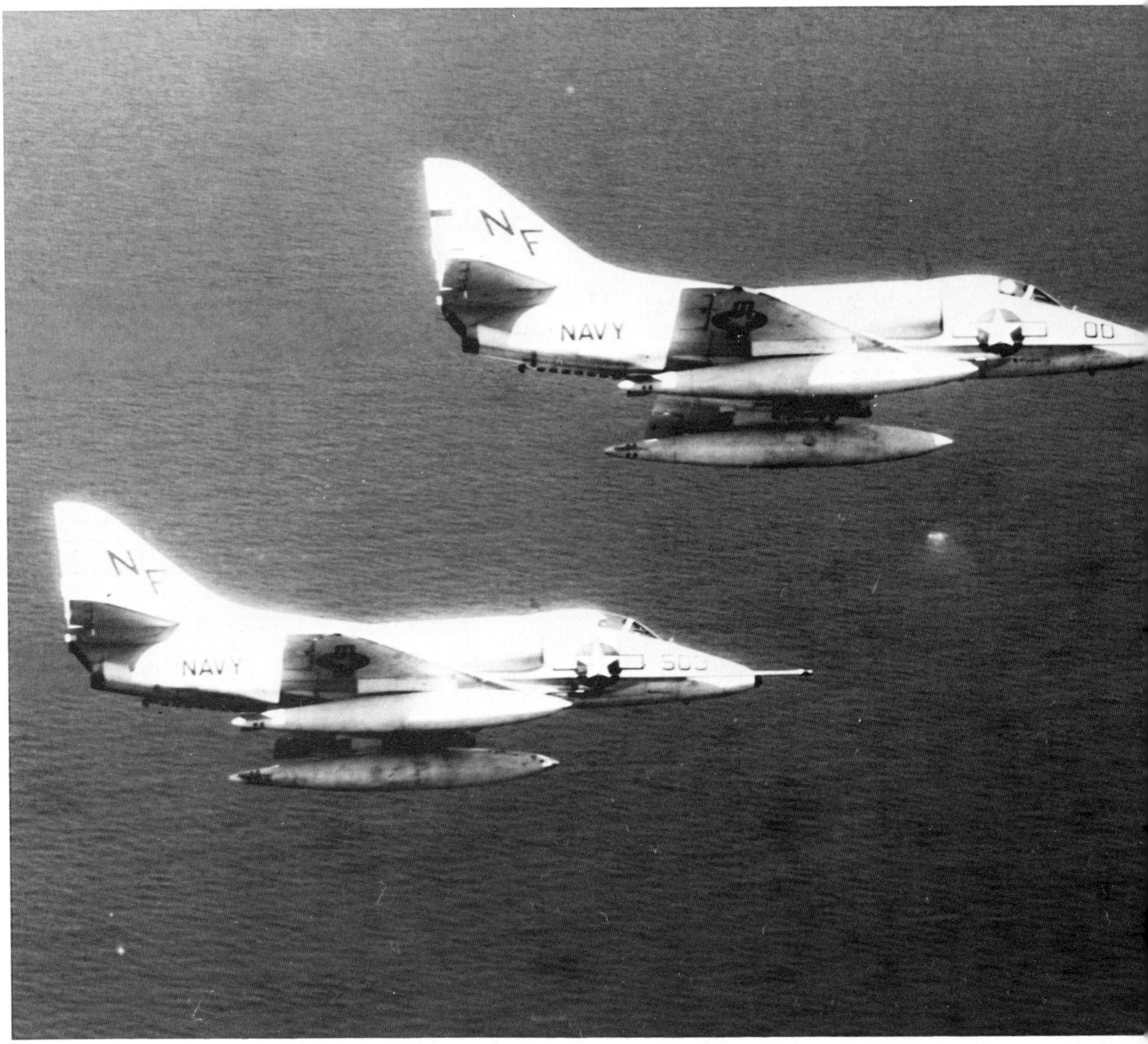
NF
NAVY
00
NF
NAVY

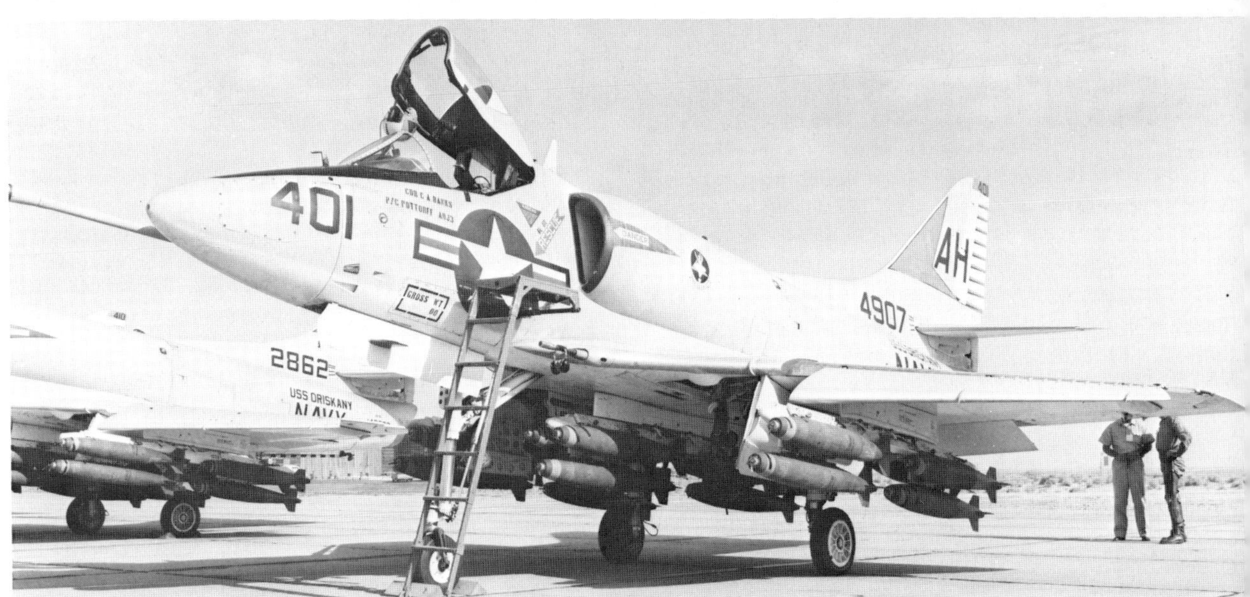

401
AH
4907
2862
USS ORISKANY

During the Vietnam War, several models of the Douglas A-4 Skyhawk series featured prominently in combat operations. Here, two A-4Bs of the 'Warhorses' VA-55 approach USS *Ticonderoga* (CVA-14) during operations in the South China Sea. The photo is dated 5 August 1964, the day aircraft from *Ticonderoga* participated in Operation Pierce Arrow, a punitive air strike on North Vietnamese bases in response to attacks on American vessels in the Tonkin Gulf. The lead aircraft in the photo bears the 'double nuts' markings of the commander of carrier air wing CVW-5, Commander W. W. Alldredge

LEFT
The potential of the Skyhawk's bomb-carrying ability is seen in this 1963 view of the A-4B (BuNo 144907) of the 'Ghost Riders' VA-164, loaded with clusters of 250-lb Mk 81 bombs. This aircraft was assigned to the commanding officer, Commander C. A. Banks, whose name is stencilled just below the windscreen. Note the RESCUE arrow, indicating the emergency cockpit release; above the English word are the Chinese characters for the same instruction. VA-164 was in combat throughout the Vietnam War, initially aboard USS *Oriskany* (CVA-34), then aboard USS *Hancock* (CVA-19)

Immediately following the second unsuccessful attack on TF 77 ships, the Pacific Fleet commander, Admiral U.S.G. Sharp Jr, recommended a punitive strike on North Vietnamese torpedo boat bases, as well as oil storage facilities at Phuc Loi and Vinh. The recommendation was approved by President Lyndon B. Johnson and on 5 August 'Operation Pierce Arrow' was launched.

Commander H.F. Griffith led the strike from USS *Constellation,* consisting of ten A-1 Skyraiders, two F-4 Phantoms and eight A-4s, against the northernmost target, the torpedo boat base at Hon Gai. Five other A-4s, as well as three F-4s and four A-1s from *Constellation* hit torpedo boat bases at Loc Chao. Simultaneously, a strike force was launched by USS *Ticonderoga's* Carrier Air Wing 5, which, through a historic coincidence, was also the first carrier air wing to see action during the Korean War. Commander R.F. Mohrhardt, commanding officer of fighter squadron VF-53, led six F-8s against the torpedo boat base at Quang Khe. The oil storage dumps at Vinh were struck by 26 other *Ticonderoga* aircraft led by then Commander (now Admiral and Commander-in-Chief of the US Atlantic Fleet) Wesley L. McDonald, commander of the A-4 squadron VA-56, and Commander W.E. Carman, skipper of the F-8 squadron VF-53. The raids were over in a matter of minutes and resulted in the near total destruction of the targets.

This early success of the A-4 also resulted in the first Skyhawk casualty of the Vietnam War. During the attack on Hon Gai, Lieutenant (junior grade) Everett Alvarez, an A-4C pilot with VA-146 from the *Constellation,* was shot down by anti-aircraft fire and taken prisoner. Lieutenant Alvarez thus became the first of nearly 600 American airmen to be held by the North Vietmanese. Their inhumane treatment of American POWs is well documented in other works and it can only be noted here that stories of such treatment were a powerful incentive to American aircrews to make every effort to bring battle-damaged aircraft back to friendly territory or, at the very least, to the Gulf of Tonkin, where rescue helicopter crews performed countless acts of heroism, picking up aircrew who bailed out or ditched.

The administration of President Johnson sought to escalate military activities in Vietnam on the 'carrot and stick' principle of hitting the enemy hard and slacking off attacks and signalling an accompanying offer to discuss reduction of hostilities. In keeping with this strategy, US forces were gradually increased, but their operations were carefully controlled by Washington, often irrespective of such factors as highest-priority targets or local weather and operating conditions.

The A-4 had quickly proved to be highly effective in combat operations in Vietnam, despite many operational restrictions. Consequently, sea-going A-4 units were augmented by land-based Skyhawk units of the US Marine Corps, which were to be used in an ever-expanding close air support role with Marine ground forces. Since there were only three airfields in South Vietnam capable of taking jets – Da Nang, Bien Hoa and Tan Son Nhut – the Marines elected to enhance their operational ability by developing a dedicated attack aircraft facility of their own. The site selected was at Chu Lai, 50 miles south of Da Nang in an easily defended location and on the sea for ease of replenishment. Using 2-foot by 12-foot sections of iron mat, a 2,000-foot-long Short Airfield for Tactical Support (SATS) was quickly put into place. The Marines are part of the American naval establishment and are therefore accustomed to the relatively short space of an aircraft carrier flight deck. Hence, the SATS facility at Chu Lai made sea-going Marine fliers feel completely at home. In addition to the short runway, mobile arresting gear was set up to capitalise on the tailhook capability of the A–4.

The first arrested landing at Chu Lai was made on 1 June 1965 by Colonel John D. Noble, commanding officer of Marine Air Group 12, followed by seven other A–4s representing advance elements of VMA–225 and VMA–311. A few hours later, Lieutenant Colonel Robert W. Baker, commanding VMA–225, led the first combat mission, leaving the field with the aid of Jet-Assisted Take-Off (JATO) equipment as the field lacked an aircraft

BELOW AND RIGHT
Navy Skyhawks also hit Viet Cong strongholds in South Vietnam. Here, Commander Robert R. King, commanding officer of the 'Black Knights' VA-23, uses his LAU-10A Zuni rocket launcher to send a salvo of five-inch folding fin rockets to the target. Commander King flew over 100 missions while his squadron was deployed aboard USS *Midway* (CVA-41) during 1965. After firing his rockets, Commander King releases a 2,000-lb Mk 84 bomb on Viet Cong forces

carrier-type catapult system. During the next eight years, the A-4s of MAG-12 proved to be a tenacious and effective adversary of Viet Cong troops in the I Corps section of South Vietnam.

On one memorable flight in January 1968, Major William E. Loftus of VMA-311 pressed his attack so close to the enemy that his A–4 quickly sustained extensive battle damage. Not wanting to come down in hostile territory and too far from the coast, Loftus headed for the Marine base at Khe Sanh and ejected over the base. His smoking Skyhawk crashed into the jungle and Loftus himself landed in the perimeter wire, where his parachute shroud lines became entangled in the barbed wire. A Marine Lieutenant and several enlisted men made their way to the perimeter and freed Loftus, who gratefully turned to the junior officer and said: 'Lieutenant, if you weren't so damned ugly, I'd kiss you.'

As early as 1965, a routine American naval presence was established in the Gulf of Tonkin. Its purpose was to keep constant pressure on the North Vietnamese, with the expectation that such pressure would retard delivery of supplies to the Viet Cong. This hub of TF77 operations was given the code name Yankee Station (a reference to the American Civil War of 1861-65 when the northern United States was called the Yankee part of the country). A few months later, a carrier position was established off the coast of South Vietnam and called Dixie Station, the complementary reference to Yankee Station. Both aircraft carrier stations gave the Americans considerable tactical flexibility in efforts to hit the south-bound flow of men and materials from North Vietnam.

The carrier-based aircraft also provided valuable photographic intelligence. On 5 April 1965, for example, an RF–8 Crusader returned to USS *Coral Sea* (CVA–43) with the first photos of a North Vietnamese surface-to-air missile (SAM) site under construction. Additional SAM sites were photographed during the following months, but back in Washington there was reluctance to have them attacked by aircraft, either carrier-based or the Navy or land-based of the Air Force. For one thing, the sites were

Among the ASW aircraft carriers in the Western Pacific during the early part of the Vietnam War was USS *Yorktown* (CVS-10), which had a detachment of A-4C aircraft from Marine attack squadron VMA-223. On 15 December 1964, First Lieutenant R. E. Enis of Detachment T made the 99,000th arrested landing aboard *Yorktown*. Incidentally, the same A-4C (BuNo 150599) made a barrier landing the day before, as shown in the photo in chapter three

En route to the combat zone, continual flight operations enhance pilot and flight deck crew efficiency. Here, an A-4C of the 'Black Diamonds' VA-216 is catapulted from USS *Hancock* (CVA-19) at the beginning of the carrier's 1965-66 deployment to the Western Pacific

undoubtedly being constructed with direct help from the Soviet Union and American political strategists were concerned that Russian technicians might be killed in any attack on incomplete sites. When the orders to attack the sites were finally approved, it was almost too late, as several American aircraft had already been brought down by the Soviet-built SAMs.

The first dedicated anti-SAM missle site effort, called Operation Iron Hand, took place on 12 August and made extensive use of the Navy's Shrike missle to identify and home-in on the SAM battery's guidance radar. Hours earlier, however, the Navy had suffered its first losses to the deadly SAMs when two A-4E Skyhawks assigned to VA-23 from USS *Midway* (CVA-41) were hit just south of Hanoi. The aircraft had been on a road reconnaissance mission when the two pilots, Lieutenant-Commander D. Roberge and his wingman, Lieutenant (junior grade) Donald H. Brown Jr, sighted two flare-like objects coming up at them. Sensing the potential danger of the unknown objects, both pilots added power and attempted to zoom away, but it was too late; the SA-2 heat-seeking missles exploded before the two A-4s could get away. Brown's aircraft was destroyed and Roberge's A-4 caught fire. In spite of the damage, Roberge managed to nurse his Skyhawk back to the *Midway*, where the underside of the aircraft was observed to be scorched and wrinkled and dotted with more than 50 holes from the explosion of the missile.

Anti-aircraft artillery (AAA) batteries and SAMs quickly became a routine menace to American aircrews operating over North Vietnam. As retired Rear Admiral E.E. (Gene) Tissot recalls, it was a highly dangerous environment in which some special features of the A-4 Skyhawk were particularly appreciated by their pilots. On the night of 18 November 1965, then Commander Tissot, commanding officer of VA-192, deployed aboard USS *Bon Homme Richard* (CVA-31), was on a mission that turned out to be anything but routine:

'My A-4C was loaded with two Bullpup-A missiles and my wingman, "Pappy" Morton, was equipped with para-flares for a little night work over the port of Quang Khe, south of Vinh. At the target area, we spotted a storage supply pier in the Song Giang River, a mile or so inland from the Tonkin Gulf. I had my wingman drop a para-flare on the other side of the target, while I made a 30-degree run from north to south, firing a Bullpup in the reflected light of the para-flare, which silhouetted the pier very well.

'I believe I hit the pier with the first Bullpup, but decided to make a second run just to make sure. Coming in again, I was surprised by a burst of anti-aircraft fire, which was the first resistance we had encountered. There was a fairly big pop and an explosion, which did a fair amount of damage to the nose of my A-4. Of course, the wiring and radar were hit, and I lost all my external and internal lights, my altimeter, angle-of-attack indicator, airspeed indicator and practically all of the cockpit instruments. My fuel gauge was spinning, so I didn't know how much fuel I still had – or whether I now had a leak.

'I immediately headed out to sea. Since my radio had

Back from the war is this A-4C of the 'Fighting Redcocks' VA-22. After landing aboard USS *Midway* (CVA-41) with his 300-gallon D-704 flight refuelling pack now dry, pilot Lieutenant (junior grade) Tom Murray provides power while a flightdeck crewman uses a tilly bar attached to the Skyhawk's nose wheel to steer the aircraft

BELOW
A-4C of the 'Mighty Shrikes' VA-94 traps number one arresting wire on USS *Hancock* (CVA-19) returning from a combat mission over North Vietnam in 1967. In the background is another Skyhawk turning onto the final approach

NE
9490
NAVY
231

A-4C of the 'Broncos' VA-112 engaged the barrier aboard USS *Kitty Hawk* (CVA-63) in the Tonkin Gulf. The aircraft, piloted by Ensign John A. Lockhard, was damaged on a strike mission, causing concern that the tailhook assembly would not take the load of an arrested landing. The flightdeck crew aboard the carrier quickly rigged the safety barrier enabling the pilot to make a safe landing

NH
3023
NH
NH

406
NAVY
NF

Two 500-lb Mk 82 bombs are loaded onto an A-4B with the specially developed Aero 46 loader

An A-4C of the 'Mighty Shrikes' VA-94 is rolled onto the deck-edge elevator of USS *Hancock* in readiness for flight operations on Yankee Station in 1967

also been knocked out, I was unable to contact my wingman, who did not know what had happened. All I could do was head in the direction of the carrier and once in the general vicinity orbit in a left-hand triangular circuit, which was the proper distress pattern to indicate to other pilots that I was lost and had no radio communications.

'A half hour or so later, about the time all of the other carrier-based planes were heading back to the ship for recovery, I was joined by an F–8 Crusader from a sister squadron. The F–8 pilot obligingly brought me down into the landing pattern, so I could make attempt to return to *Bon Homme Richard.*

'So, there I was with no lights and no radio contact. It was a clear, moonless night and I could see the ship alright. I had a bit of trouble vectoring around the landing pattern, but I could see the ship downwind and sensed they knew I had some sort of an emergency condition and, therefore, were accommodating me in the pattern. But with no angle-of-attack or airspeed indicators, I soon found how difficult it was to achieve the proper approach speed. You certainly develop a feel for what the proper airspeed is by virtue of all the previous carrier landings you have made, but when you don't have any instruments at all, it's difficult to get the speed right on the mark. As it turned out, I was about 15 or 20 knots too fast – and I wasn't about to get too slow!

NP
1102
NAVY

Skyhawk durability is seen in this view of an A-4E of the 'Rampant Raiders' VA-212 from USS *Bon Homme Richard* (CVA-31). During an air strike over North Vietnam on 25 April 1967, Lieutenant (junior grade) Alan Crebo's aircraft was hit by ground fire, knocking off the rudder and starting a fire at the junction of the fuselage and wing. Despite the damage, Crebo headed back to the carrier. His wingman, Lieutenant Graham, took this photo when Crebo tried to lower the landing gear ; only the nose wheel and tailhook dropped, ruling out any hopes for a carrier landing. The pilot later ejected near the carrier, and was rescued by helicopter

A-4E of the 'Blue Blazers' VA-93 streaks by the flight deck of USS *Hancock* (CVA-19) after receiving a 'wave off' from the landing signal officer. The aircraft, just back from a combat mission, carries AGM-45A Shrike anti-radiation missiles on launch rails outboard of the 150-gallon fuel tanks

Consequently, I was close to the maximum speed allowed to engage the arresting gear.

'On my first attempt at landing, I "boltered" (missed the arresting gear) and continued around for another pass. I was high and fast on that one – and boltered the next time, as well. As best I could tell, I was slowing the plane down on each successive pass, but on the third attempt I was waved off for still being too fast.

'On the fourth pass, I knew I didn't have a great deal of fuel left. My fuel gauge was still spinning, but I knew that if I'd had a fuel leak, I'd long since have run out of fuel. So, knowing how long I'd been airborne and what I'd been doing. I calculated I was down to around 1,000 pounds of fuel, which is getting to be a low fuel state in the A–4. I came around on what I thought was a pretty good pass and, again, got the flashing red lights indicating a wave-off.

'I later learned that this pass *was* good and I probably would have gotten aboard with no problem. However, it seems that someone in the large crowd of spectators that had assembled in "Pri-Fly" (the Air Officer's flight station in the island superstructure, from which all flight operations are controlled) to watch the show had inadvertently put his hand on the wave-off button as I was coming in on my final approach!

'As I pulled up again, an A–4 tanker appeared, nicely positioned in front of me. I got the message and took advantage of this opportunity to refuel the airplane. I had trouble getting the landing gear up, but finally did it by pressing the override switch in the landing gear handle; that trouble was no doubt an electrical problem due to the damage sustained by the AAA fire.

'Just as I was able to retract the gear and was almost certain my fuel state was so low that I'd "flame out" any second – just then, the nose cone of the airplane blew back. It was hinged at the top and so it just flipped up 180 degrees and stayed right on top of the nose of the airplane, like a big airscoop. Of course, I couldn't radio the tanker pilot about my difficulty and he couldn't see me because he was ahead of me. Even using full power and all of my precious fuel, I wouldn't have been able to plug into him with all that extra drag on the nose.

'All I could do at this point was to lower the seat and put the plane in a dive at full power. I went whistling past the tanker and he had enough sense to keep me in sight. In my dive from about 5,000 feet – going at about 400 knots – the radome blew off, leaving me with a blunt nose, but lot less drag. After three or four stabs, I was able to get plugged in to the tanker. Then the tanker pilot, Ole Olson from VA–195, our sister squadron, took me into our divert airfield at Da Nang, where I successfully concluded the longest, most tiring flight I'd ever had.' During his 36-year career, Admiral Tissot became the third Navy pilot to achieve 1,000 carrier landings.

Admiral Tissot's base of operations with VA–192, USS *Bon Homme Richard,* was but one of several World War II vintage *Essex*-class carriers that proved the continuing effectiveness of those ships. The 'Bonnie Dick', as she was affectionately known, saw action in World War II and the Korean War prior to being assigned to Yankee Station during much of the Vietnam War. The relatively small-

A-4F of the 'Warhorses' VA-55 fires an AGM-45A Shrike air-to-surface missile which is designed to home in on enemy radar emissions

BELOW LEFT
A camera mounted on the underside of the fuselage of the A-4E flown by Lieutenant (junior grade) James L. Steel of VA-55 shows a Bullpup missile streaking towards a bridge 33 miles south of Hanoi, North Vietnam

BELOW
Second in the sequence shows the missile to have perfectly found its mark. This action is dated October 1967. At the time, VA-55 was commanded by Commander (later Rear Admiral) Robert E. Kirksey, who selected Lieutenant Steel to be his wingman

Commander W. H. Robinson, commanding officer of the 'Roadrunners' VA-144, on a routine flight over California in 1968. The absence of a ship identification on the aircraft indicates the squadron was at the time on an 'in port' status

JET
INTAKE
RESCUE
301

deck *Essex*-class ships (with flight decks just under 1,000 feet long) later became less effective for the bigger heavier and faster jets in use, but were nearly the ideal launching platforms for the smaller, lighter A–4 variants.

In August 1965, another Pacific combat veteran of World War II, USS *Hornet* (CVS–12), left San Diego, California for renewed use as a combat vessel off Vietnam. *Hornet's* air wing had been restructured and her role had been changed from attack aircraft carrier (CVA) to anti-submarine warfare aircraft carrier (CVS). Her ASW air group was seen as the counter to the potential threat that North Vietnam's communist bloc allies might provide submarines for use against US ships at Yankee Station.

Hornet's ASW sonar-bearing helicopters and submarine-tracking fixed-wing aircraft found no opposition beneath the waters of Tonkin Gulf, but the availability of another carrier flight deck off the coast of Vietnam was not overlooked by American naval tacticians. Thus, in October and November, Skyhawks from Marine Corps headquarters and maintenance squadron H&MS–15 on USS *Midway* were deployed aboard *Hornet.* the Marine A–4s primarily attacked Viet Cong forces in South Vietnam and in that two-month period the four-plane detachment dropped 84 tons of ordnance and expended 7,400 rounds of 20mm ammunition in 108 sorties. In addition to their basic attack capability, the Marine A–4s were also available of flying Combat Air Patrol (CAP) missions to intercept enemy aircraft that might attack *Hornet*-based ASW aircraft.

The flexibility of temporarily deploying A–4s aboard

A-4E of the 'Rampant Raiders' VA-212 is readied for take-off from USS *Bon Homme Richard* (CVA-31) during combat operations in June 1968. Mounted under the wings are Sidewinder (right), and Shrike missiles and 1,000-lb Mk 83 bombs

ASW aircraft carriers proved so appealing that, in April 1966, the Atlantic Fleet-based USS *Intrepid* (CVS–11) off-loaded her normal air wing and took aboard Carrier Air Wing 10 for a combat deployment to Vietnam. CVW–10 initially comprised squadrons of A–1, A–4 and F–8 aircraft, but by the third combat cruise, in 1968, the air wing was made up of three A–4 squadrons, with one F–8 squadron to provide CAP.

The last of the *Essex*-class aircraft carriers to enter service, USS *Oriskany* (CVA–34), was the sea-going home for for a number of A–4 squadrons during the Vietnam War. On 23 July 1966, the petroleum, oil and lubricants (POL) storage facility at Vinh was attacked by Carrier Air Wing 16 aircraft from *Oriskany*. The ruggedness of the Skyhawk proved to be a lifesaver to Commander Wynne F. Foster, commanding officer of VA–163, whose A–4E took a 57mm AAA shell through the starboard side of the cockpit. The shell severed Commander Foster's right arm just below the shoulder. Trying to restrict the loss of blood by holding the stump of his shattered arm with his left, the A–4 pilot steered his aircraft by using his knees. He spotted the guided missile frigate USS *Reeves* (DLG–24) and, when near enough to the friendly ship, Commander Foster managed to use his left hand to activate his ejection seat. He was picked up by the frigate's crew and evacuated to the carrier, where emergency surgery was performed.

Commander Foster was succeeded in command of VA–163 by Commander Ron Caldwell, while to fill the executive officer's billet, an experienced senior A–4 pilot from VA–66 was transferred to the unit. That officer, now

A-4E of the 'Gladiators' VA-106 is tied down near the starboard catapult of USS *Intrepid* (CVS-11) during July 1968 operations off Yankee Station. If needed, it can be quickly untied, positioned and catapulted into action

RIGHT
On the catapult and ready to go, this A-4E of the 'Gladiators' VA-106 receives final check from flightdeck crewman just prior to launching from USS *Intrepid* (CVS-11) during Tonkin Gulf operations in 1968

retired Rear Admiral Bryan W. Compton, subsequently led the squadron through some of the most difficult aerial operations of the war. His own role was recognised by the presentation to him of the Navy cross, the second highest American award for valour.

The conclusion of then-Commander Compton's latter half of the 1966 cruise was marred by a disastrous fire aboard *Oriskany* on 26 October. The 44 officers and enlisted men killed in the fire included four VA–163 squadron-mates. A number of aircraft were also destroyed or damaged in the fire.

'The following July,' Admiral Compton recalls, 'we were back in the Tonkin Gulf after some personnel turn-over and a heavy training period, still aboard *Oriskany*. We got to Yankee Station just as the tempo of operations had picket up. The campaign had changed emphasis from armed reconnaissance to large strikes on fixed targets of the North Vietnamese infrastructure.

'As we had fitted out and trained to handle the Walleye (television-guided air-to-surface glide bomb), we knew we would get our share of the targets. We slid rapidly into a three-major-strikes-a-day campaign, occassionally broken by a return to cyclic recce flights. We called it the "Doctor Pepper 10-2-4 Schedule" because of the regularity. We thought we were a pretty shaken down outfit with lots of experience, but the level of opposition – AAA and SAMs – exceeded anything we had seen before. Although we were hitting the targets pretty hard, we were paying a stiff price. Before the first month of operations was over, we had lost close to ten pilots from the Air Wing. With a hundred pilots in the Wing, the arithmetic didn't seem good, but I think everyone felt he wasn't included in the odds.

'Early in August we got orders to plan a strike on the Hanoi power plant using our Walleye's. Commander Homer Smith, skipper of VA-212, had led the first strike on the power plant in May, but it was still in operation and a juicy target. As I had relieved Ron Caldwell just before the start of the cruise, I got to lead the strike.

'We planned to coast in from the south until we were just west of a line between Phu Ly and Hanoi and just south of the range of Hanoi's major SAM batteries. From this point, we would turn our A–4s north to Hanoi, fanning out about 25 miles from the target, which was on the north-west edge of the city. We planned for five Walleye drops to execute a simultaneous network coming from the west counter-clockwise to the south-south-east. We thought this approach would give each of us a chance to release the weapon on his individual aim point and still dilute the defences by the simultaneity of the attack.

'Even though the main part of the plant was large, we

AK
2069
NAVY
207

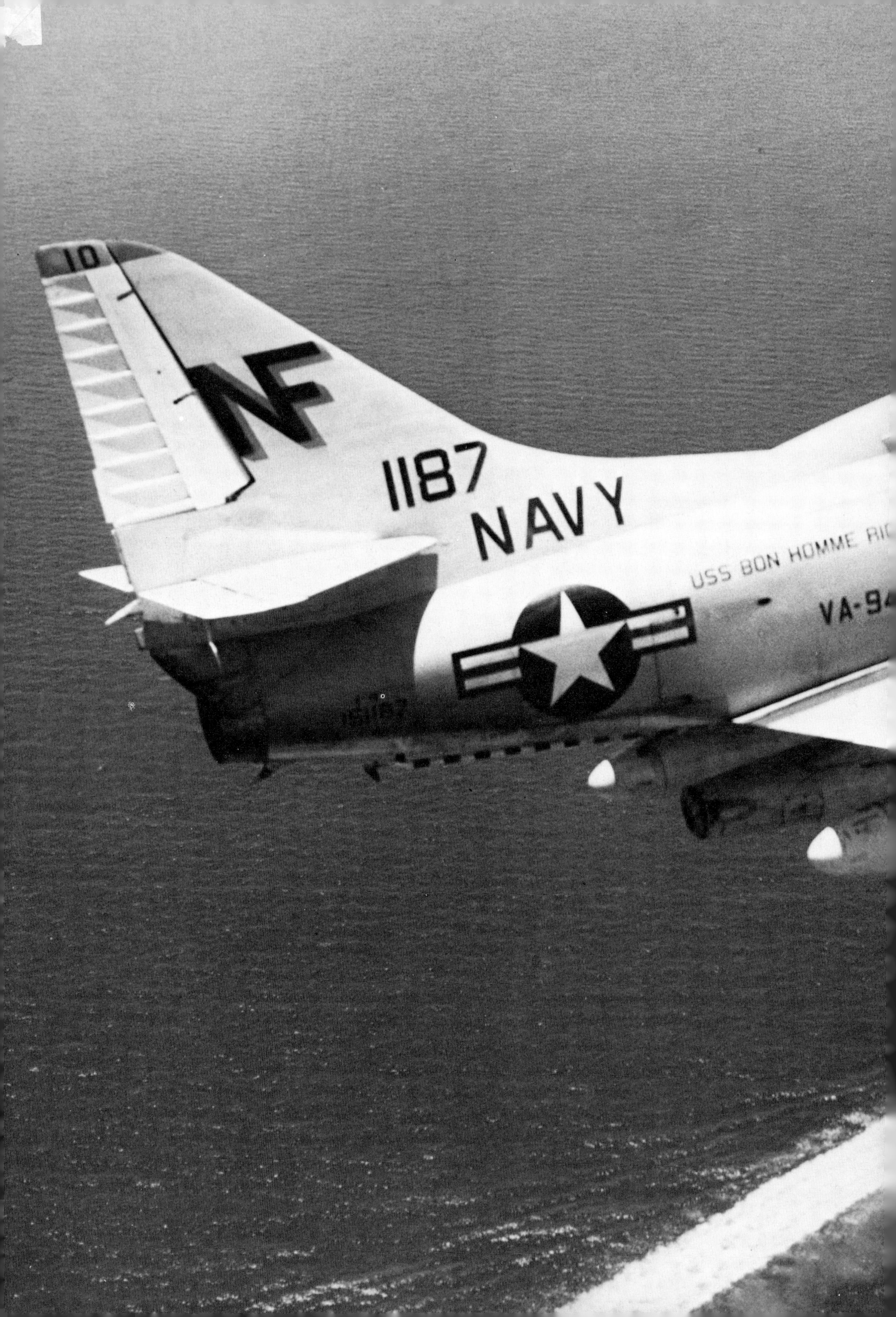

10
NF
1187
NAVY
USS BON HOMME RI
VA-94

Lieutenant (junior grade) Bob Gastin in an A-4E of the 'Mighty Shrikes' VA-94 passes over USS *Bon Homme Richard* (CVA-31) in the Tonkin Gulf. The aircraft is equipped with the D-704 flight refuelling pack and orbiting the ship ready to refuel returning aircraft

TOP
A-4C of the 'Bombing Broncos' VA-112 engages arresting gear aboard USS *Kitty Hawk* (CVA-63) following combat operations over North Vietnam in January 1968

ABOVE RIGHT
Lieutenant (junior grade) Jack Thomas brings his A-4C of the 'Roadrunners' VA-144 back aboard USS *Kitty Hawk* (CVA-63) in the Tonkin Gulf during April 1968

ABOVE
Paveway laser-guided Mk 84 2,000-lb bomb carried on a US Marine Corps A-4 at NAS Point Mugu, California test facility. A family of so-called 'smart bombs' were developed for A-4s and other attack aircraft during the Vietnam War

RIGHT
Commander Bill Greiwe, commander of carrier air group CVG-21, moves forward on the port catapult of USS *Hancock* (CVA-19). The air group commander often flew several different aircraft types, reflecting the composition of the air group, and in this case Commander Greiwe is in an A-4F in the markings of the 'Rampant Raiders' VA-212

were concerned that smoke and dust from the impact of the first weapon might decoy the others. We were anxious to get as close to simultaneous impact as possible. Since we were coming in essentially together, this required some careful adjustment of speed and manoeuvring. We were not using any flak suppression on the strike for the final attack, so we rejected the option of dropping the weapons sequentially.

'After we put together our plan, we brief *Oriskany's* skipper, Captain Billy D. Holder, then rear Admiral Walter L. Curtis Jr, Commander of Carrier Division 9, and then Rear Admiral Mehle, Commander of Task Force 77. Once they were satisfied with the plan, we returned to our recce and major strike effort until a date was set for the Walleye raid.

'I was out on a recce hop with Lieutenant Ken Adams, my regular wingman, and was looking for a target for him, as I had dropped all my bombs. Just as Ken rolled in for his final run, I got tagged by a 37mm round as I circled the area. The round blew away the outboard half of the port aileron. The control was sluggish, but I still had control of the aircraft. We headed back to the ship, but decided to go to Chu Lai to get the plane fixed.

'I really felt disgusted with myself at this stage. I felt I got hit because I had gotten complacent, thinking I was in a safe area at Branden Bay, I wasn't jinking hard. I was concerned that the Hanoi strike would come up and that I would be stranded ashore. All these thoughts flashed through my mind as I landed at Chu Lai. I couldn't have gotten better support. The Marines of MAG-12 said they would change the aileron and have the plane ready to go in the morning. The marine Master Sergeant was as good as his word; the plane was loaded and ready the next day. When I got back to the ship, I found the Hanoi strike was on for the following day, November 21.

'On the morning of the strike, we were up early for our last-minute briefing. Since we were only dropping one Walleye each, we slicked up the airplanes, taking off the 400-gallon centre-line auxiliary fuel tanks and the two triple ejector racks (TERs) on the inboard wing stations. Since we wanted to be topped off (attain maximum fuel state), we planned to refuel en route to our coast-in point. The only cover we had was a Target Combat Air Patrol (TARCAP) that went into our turn point south of Hanoi and two "Iron Hand" aircraft dropped off at the same basic position.

'The briefing, launch and rendezvous went smoothly. As we really didn't have a big gaggle, it was a piece of cake. Crossing the beach, topped off, and with just one weapon, we were really scooting along. Indeed, we got to the turn point without a single SAM being fired at us. As we had had some SAMs fired at us on previous strikes near Hanoi, I was really surprised at how quiet it was this time. It didn't last long. As we turned, two SAMs came up at us from south of Hanoi. There wasn't to be a break until the strike was over some 15 minutes later.

'Our flight was moving around well in a loose formation, jinking heavily. For me, at least, the adrenalin was up and I was all eyeballs. The rest of the strike group – Lieutenant-Commanders Jim Busey, Dean Cramer, Jerry

5
NM
3
NM
7712
NAVY

Two A-4Cs of the 'Dambusters' VA-195 en route to USS *Bon Homme Richard* (CVA-31)

Lieutenant Commander (subsequently Captain) Michael J. Estocin of the 'Golden Dragons' VA-192 was the only A-4 pilot to receive the Medal of Honor, the highest American award for valor. The award was made posthumously, as it is now believed he did not survive his final heroic mission on 26 April 1967

RIGHT
Commander (later Rear Admiral) E. E. Tissot standing by the A-4C he flew as commanding officer of the 'Golden Dragons' VA-192 aboard USS *Bon Homme Richard* (CVA-31) in 1965. Commander Tissot was awarded the Silver Star with gold star in lieu of a second award, the DFC with four gold stars, the Air Medal with five gold stars and the Navy Commendation Medal with four gold stars and the Combat V for his combat service with VA-192. Later promoted to command carrier air wing CVW-14 aboard USS *Constellation* (CVA-64), he was awarded the Legion of Merit for planning and coordinating major air strikes against North Vietnam. He personally led 23 strikes

A-4C of the 'War Eagles' ASW fighter squadron VSF-1 about to land aboard USS *Independence* (CVA-62) in the Mediterranean during 1968. To bolster the defensive power of ASW air groups, four units were formed – VSF-1 and VSF-3 as active units, VSF-76 and VSF-86 as reserve units – to use the A-4C in a role similar to fighter cover. The concept did not last long. VSF-1 was commissioned in July 1965 and decommissioned in January 1970

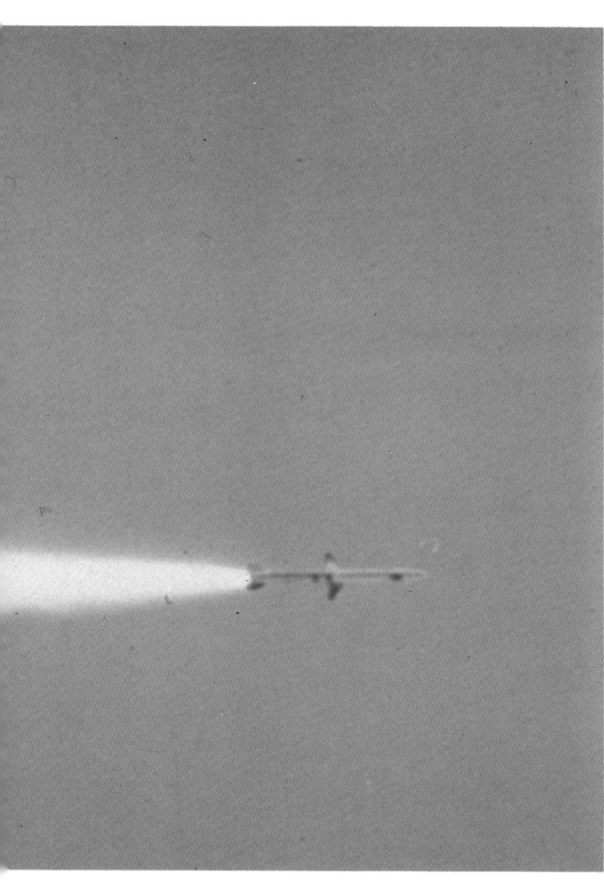

A-4E of the 'Warhorses' VA-55 fires an AGM-45A Shrike air-to-surface missile over California test range prior to 1969-70 deployment to Yankee Station aboard USS *Hancock* (CVA-19)

BELOW LEFT
A-4 Skyhawk of carrier air wing CVW-6 are catapulted in rapid succession from what was then the latest US carrier, USS *America* (CVA-66), in the Mediterranean during June 1967. Earlier that year, *America* was used for the carrier suitability trials of the LTV A-7A Corsair II, the intended successor of the A-4

BELOW
A-4C Skyhawk of the 'Sunliners' VA-81 is readied for early evening launch from USS *John F. Kennedy* (CVA-67), while on its Caribbean shake down cruise in November 1968. On the 22nd October that year Commander Hal L. Marr, commanding carrier air wing CVW-1, made the first landing aboard the *JFK* in an A-4C

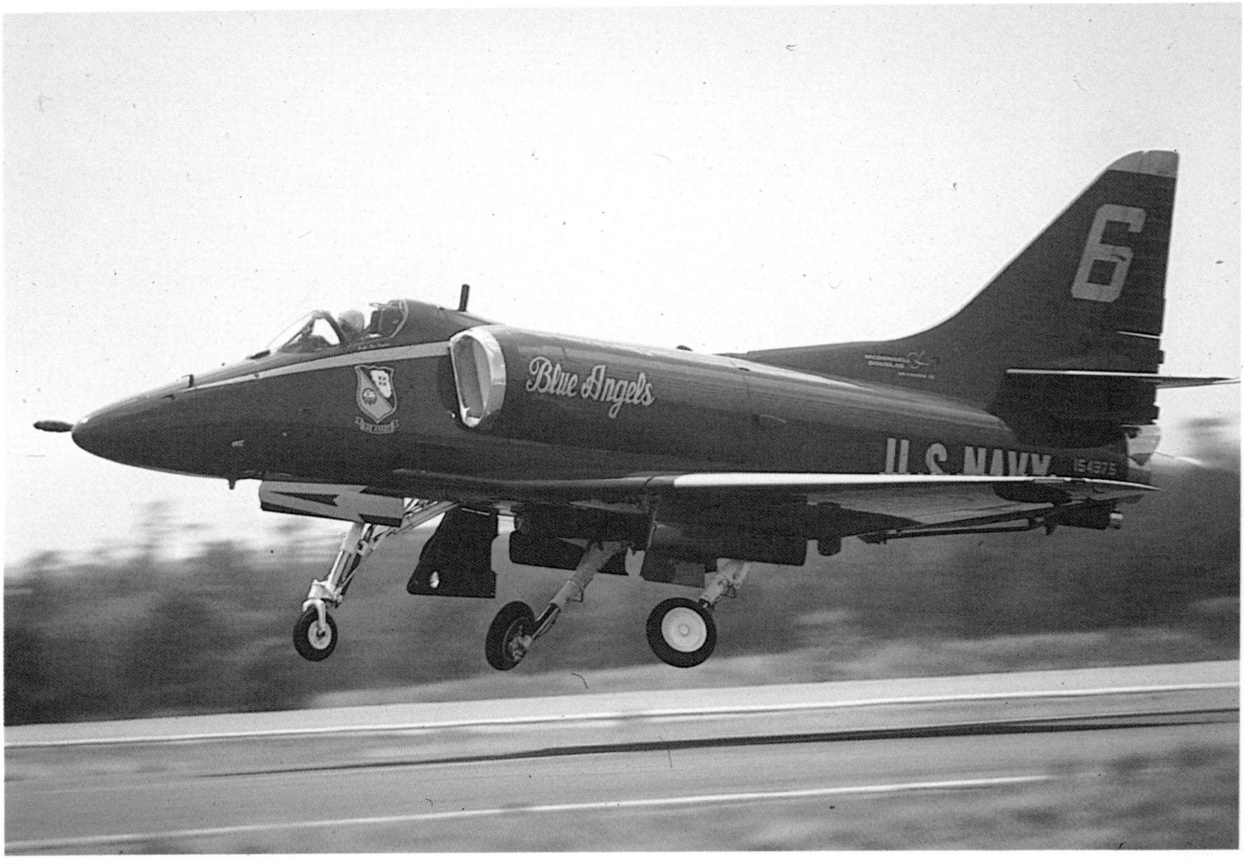
6
Blue Angels
U.S. NAVY

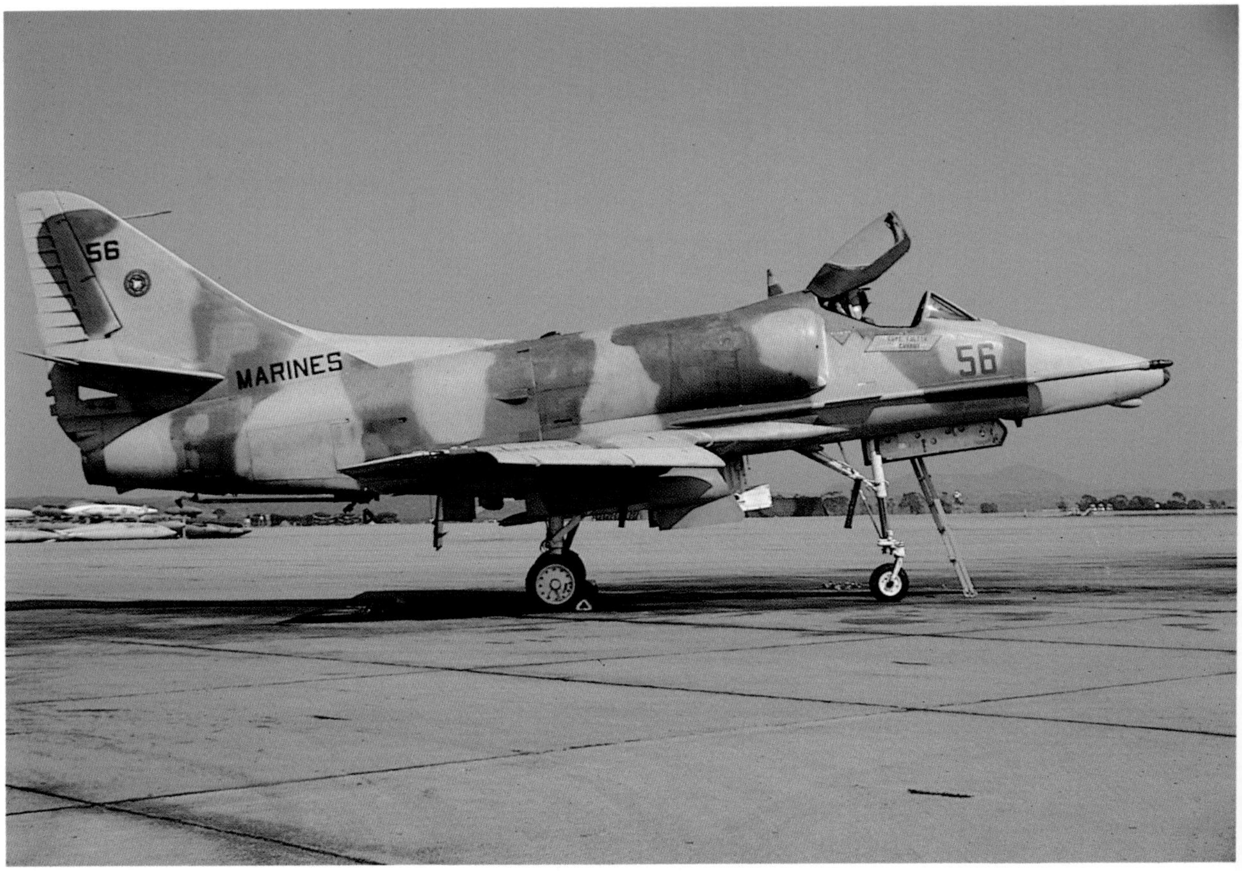
56
MARINES
56

LEFT
Distinctive navy blue and gold colour scheme of the U.S. Navy's 'Blue Angels' flight demonstration team gives instant recognition to this specially-modified A-4F Skyhawk

BELOW LEFT
Used in 'Top Gun' exercises from NAS Miramar. This A-4F of VF-126 aggressor squadron, is painted in Soviet-style camouflage and markings

RIGHT
Two A-4M Skyhawks of the 'Tomcats' US Marine Corps attack squadron VMA-311 show both the new, two-tone grey colour scheme and the earlier light grey and white with squadron colours. VMA-311, which began using Skyhawks in 1958, was one of the last American combat units to leave Vietnam, after eight years of continous service

BELOW
A-4K Skyhawk of No. 75 Squadron, Royal New Zealand Air Force, in the green and brown camouflage scheme that has since replaced the standard light grey and white that was once used on most Skyhawks, even export aircraft

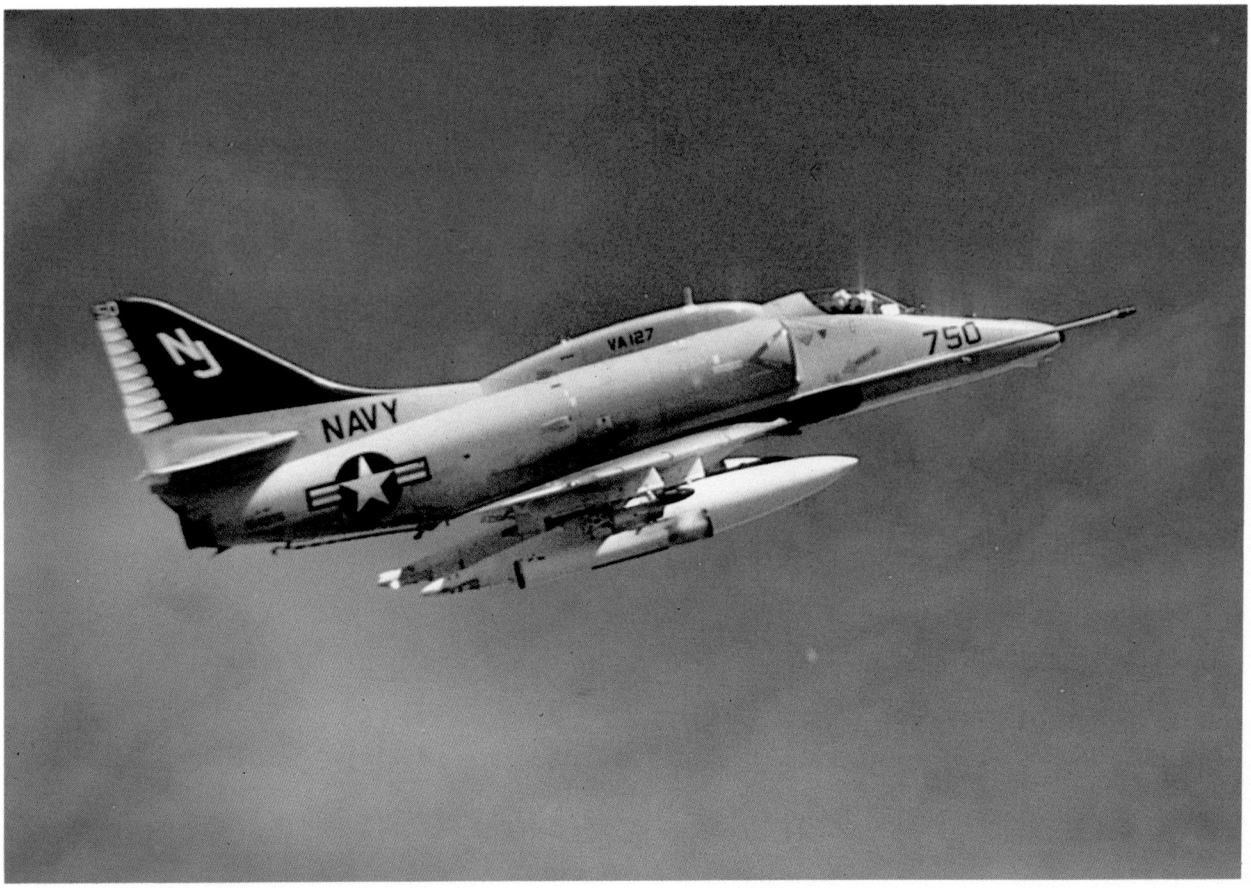

NAVY
502
NAVY
00

UA
4632
NAVY
02

A-4G Skyhawk of the 'Checkmates' VF-805 Squadron of the Royal Australian Navy taxies at Nowra, New South Wales

ABOVE LEFT
A Skyhawk of the 'Batmen' VA-127 on a training mission. VA-127 became A-4 readiness air group RAG-12 in 1962, after the previous holder of that designation, VA-126, was recomissioned as fighter squadron VF-126

FAR LEFT
Outward bound on a bombing mission, two A-4Es of the 'Warhorses' VA-55 carry mixed weapon loads. Aircraft 502 has six bombs and two Bullpup missiles, 00 has six bombs and two Zuni rocket pods. Both carry two external fuel tanks

Fleet composite squadrons continue to make wide use of Skyhawks. Here, an A-4E (BuNo 150056) of the 'Unique Antiques' VC-1 lets out its refuelling drogue to one of the squadron's brightly decorated TA-4J aircraft (BuNo 154632) over Hawaii. Such colourful schemes once widely used in U.S. naval aviation, are now giving way to two-tone grey to make aircraft less visible to potential adversaries

A-4N Skyhawk II aircraft produced for Israel's *Heyl Ha'Avir* were painted in a unique three-tone camouflage scheme. Shown here on a test flight over California; the national markings were not applied by Douglas

Breast and Vance Schoefeldt – were top aviators and really steady aces. Generally, the strike frequency (on the radio) is filled with chatter. Now the only thing you heard was the code call for a SAM that really threatened the strike group. Occasionally, we would have a disagreement in the Wing on this point – i.e. the "no threat" call – but not with this group of professionals.

'As we fanned out for our run-in, we could see Hanoi clearly: the Dourmer Bridge across the Red River, the triangular lake on the northwest side of the city, next the the power plant, and the plant itself. I had the westerly run-in and, as I arced around the city, I could see flashes of light as the AAA batteries opened fire. They seemed to be concentrating on the southern approach.

'Locking now on the target, I got a good picture of the west front of the power plant on my gunsight. Shifting to the Sony Scope (small television screen to monitor the Walleye's flight to the target), I could see the cross-hair locked on a window in the face of the building, so I "pickled" the weapon away. For some reason nobody seemed to be tracking me with their guns now, so as I pulled away, I took a turn around the target and tried to get a picture or two with my hand-held camera. I could see three distinct impacts on the power plant, but could not see the other two.

'Jim Busey and Dean Cramer, who had made their run-in from the south side, had had a tough time. Both had gotten hit and had managed to get their weapons off only with great difficulty. As we returned to the ship, we were very much elated, for we knew we had hit a good target really hard. At the same time, we were very much concerned about both Jim and Dean. When we finally landed on the ship and got a chance to see the hole in Dean's plane, it was big enough for a man to stand up in, with his body coming through the hole in the wing.'

The Walleye attack on the Hanoi thermal power plant is one of the noteworthy successes of the A–4 in combat. Another interesting account of Rear Admiral Compton's exceptional performance during the Vietnam War is related by his friend Rear Admiral Robert E. Kirksey, who was skipper of VA–55, deployed alternately aboard USS *Hancock* (CVA–19) and USS *Constellation.* Commenting on the frustration of having to avoid certain targets because of the presence of vessels flying the flags of neutral countries, Kirksey notes that Compton had a creative – if hazardous – approach to dealing with the problem:

'We were not allowed to hit certain bridges linking main supply routes into Haiphong, because third-country shipping was tied up at piers nearby. We were only permitted to go after one of these bridges when it had been ascertained that there was no potential for hitting third-country shipping.

'On one occasion, Bryan Compton was going in after one of these bridges when he received a message saying there was a report that third-country shipping was right near the bridge. So, he diverted to another target and dropped his bombs on it. He still had in mind to hit that bridge, however, and wanted to be sure just where the third-country shipping was tied up – so that, when it was gone, he'd be able to take out the bridge.

'At this point, it was late in the day and it was getting pretty dark down on the ground. Before heading back for his ship, Bryan wanted to be certain just which vessels were near the bridge, so he went down for a good close look. He came in low, dropped his landing gear, turned on his landing lights and flew slowly along the waterfront, trying to read the names on the sterns of the ships tied up. There he was, with his gear down, flaps down, eyeballing these ships, while every gunner on the ground was going crazy trying to draw a bead on such a low target. And that, of course, was the secret of his success: nobody ever expected an airplane to come so close to his objective.

'Bryan was absolutely fearless in combat and so, when he went down like that, he usually got what he wanted. I think the North Vietnamese must have thought he was something like the Red Baron – just a totally fearless and invulnerable character who could do those things and get away with them. I'm sure after a while, the enemy must have figured out that these "Comptonisms" were just another part of the war they'd have to endure.'

Admiral Kirksey, whose own exploits earned him the Silver Star, the third highest American award for valour, knew and worked with a number of pilots in whose hands the A–4 was a most effective instrument of war. One of these was then-Lieutenant (junior grade) James L. Steel.

'He was a newly "nuggeted" ensign when he joined my squadron and one who took very well to aviation', Kirksey recalls. 'We assigned the new pilots to be wingmen for the more experienced people, to give them a chance to become seasoned with some very skilled people, and I was so impressed with Ensign Steel that I selected him as my wingman.

'Refining his skills in the A–4, Jim Steel soon developed into a first-rate naval aviator. I never had any qualms about getting on his wing if anything happened to my radio on the way back to the ship at night, which happened from time to time. I would temporarily lose my TACAN or my radio and then just slide on Jim's wing and stay there until he started flickering his lights, which meant I was all lined up to come aboard the carrier. If I happened to come in a bit high and "boltered", I'd keep right on going and, once I'd gotten up to about 400 feet, I could look up to the 10 o'clock position and see Jim, waiting to bring me around again. We didn't always have that much confidence in all the newer pilots, but Jim was truly exceptional.

'At some point in training for our Vietnam combat cruise, Jim picked up the nickname "Iron Man". Once we began operating off Yankee Station, Jim proved to be a really iron-steady pilot. When we would go out on "Iron Hand" missions (to attack SAM sites), our routine was that Jim would concentrate on the target, while I would search the sky, looking for SAMs or enemy fighters. Many times there would be considerable AAA fire coming up at us, but Jim would concentrate on his target and not let his Shrike missiles go until he knew he would score. Then, typcially, he would look around and see signs of all the AAA fire coming at us and say; "Wow, look at that! Let's get the hell out of here, skipper."

As Admiral Kirksey noted, in addition to AAA fire and SAMs, there was an ever-present danger of enemy figher aircraft appearing. At the beginning of hostilities, the

North Vietnamese Air Force was equipped with a relatively small number of old MiG-15 fighter aircraft of the Korean War period. They were clearly no match for the more modern, missile-equipped fighters used by the US Navy and Air Force. However, the North Vietnamese were quickly provided with newer aircraft – including MiG-17, -19 and -21 fighters – and the necessary training to acquaint pilots with the high-speed environment of modern aerial combat.

While the Skyhawk has been equipped with defensive weapons, the aircraft was not intended to fill the fighter role. Consequently, there is to date only one known instance of a US Navy A–4 shooting down an enemy fighter aircraft over Vietnam – and it is an interesting tribute to the flexibility of this primarily attack-orientated aircraft.

On 1 May 1967, aircraft from Carrier Air Wing 21 deployed aboard USS *Bon Homme Richard* were assigned to attack Kep Airfield, outside Hanoi. Lieutenant-Commander Theodore R. Swartz, flying an A–4C of VA–76, was firing Zuni rockets at two MiGs on the runway when a fellow pilot radioed to alert him to two airborne enemy fighters at his 'six o'clock' position (directly behind him in the classic dogfight 'kill' position).

'I spotted the attacking aircraft and put my A–4 into a high barrel roll, dropping in behind the MiGs', Swartz recalled. 'From this markedly advantageous position, I fired several air-to-ground rockets at the Number Two MiG and then got another call that there was a MiG at my six o'clock (position) again. I was not able to see my rockets hit as I bent my A–4 hard, checking for the suspected third MiG.'

Commander Swartz's wingman saw the enemy fighter, a MiG-17, hit the ground, thereby confirming the only recorded A–4 MiG kill of the Vietnam War.

VA–76's attack on Kep Airfield was part of a broadening of target opportunities in 1967. Recognizing that electrical power, as well as petroleum, oil and lubricants (POL) stores were highly important to the North Vietnamese war effort, more of those facilities were classified by Washington as acceptable targets. They were difficult targets to hit, but that difficulty was largely overcome by the manoeuvreable A–4.

On 20 April 1967, Lieutenant-Commander Michael J. Estocin led a three-plane group of VA-192 Skyhawks from USS *Ticonderoga* against two thermal power plants in Haiphong. Throughout the mission, Estocin alerted his strike group leaders when SAMs were launched against them. He also destroyed three of the SAM launching sites on his own, during the course of which his A–4 was damaged by a missile.

Estocin pulled away from the target area, assessed that heavy damage to the aircraft had not affected the A–4's major flight systems, and re-entered the area to launch another Shrike missle attack. He had fuel for less than five minutes more in the air when he finally flew away from Haiphong. Fortunately, a tanker aircraft was able to supply enough fuel to get him close enough for one carrier approach. His badly damaged A–4 caught fire as he came in, but Estocin managed to bring it back.

Four days later, while leading an attack on POL facilities in Haiphong, Estocin again turned his attention to the SAM sites and again his aircraft took heavy damage from an exploding missile. Even though his A–4 was on fire this time, he got the aircraft under control and returned to launch another Shrike missile before leaving the area.

Lieutenant-Commander Estocin did not return to USS *Ticonderoga* this time. Initially, he was listed as missing in action on 26 April 1967, after being forced down in enemy territory. On 10 November 1977, his status was changed to presumed killed in action. On 27 February 1978, the A–4 pilot (promoted to Captain during the years before his status was clarified) was honoured with the posthumous award of the Medal of Honour, the highest American military decoration for valour. At the presentation ceremony in Washington, Captain Estocin's uncommon courage and devotion to duty were further marked when his widow was also presented with the Distinguished Flying Cross, Air Medal, Navy Commendation Medal and Purple Heart (the latter for wounds suffered in combat) that he had also earned.

Two final comments serve to demonstrate the confidence A–4 pilots had in their aircraft as a weapons delivery system under the most adverse conditions.

Lieutenant Hart 'Irish' Schwarzenbach of VA–94, after a raid on Vinh in 1967, recalled: 'We were hitting a well-defended target and I was flying as the fourth man in the slot. Right after my roll-in, my plane was hit in the left wing; it inverted completely. All I could think about was the downtown dance in Vinh and how I was going to be a participant.

'It took a bit of strain to right the plane, but the Skyhawk was still up there and would not give in. I could see from the reflection on the ground that it was streaming a trail of fuel, making me a good target. An A-3 Skywarrior tanker picked me up at the coastline and pumped fuel to the engine all the way to the ship, where, even with a hole blasted in the wing, I made a nice easy landing (That is why) when A–4 pilots get together in the Ready Room and talk about missions and taking hits, somebody has a new story about an A-4 that stayed in the air when, in theory, it shouldn't have been able to fly.'

Lieutenant (junior grade) Roger Van Dyke of VA-93 sums up what many Skyhawk pilots have expressed: 'The A–4 is only 40 feet long and has a wing spread of less than 30 feet, but its weapons delivery system, its speed, its manoeuvreability and its determination to stay in the air under adverse circumstances – coupled with a pilot's own determination – is a great combination for combat flying.'

A-4E of the 'Valions' VA-15 comes in for a landing aboard USS *Intrepid* (CVS-11), an ASW carrier *temporarily* reassigned as a light attack aircraft carrier for three combat cruises to Vietnam. The LTV F-8C Crusader (No.17) parked off the flight line is that of Lieutenant Tony Nargi of the 'Sundowners' VF-111 who, on 19 September 1968, shot down a North Vietnamese MiG-21

5
In Foreign Skies

In addition to nicely fitting American requirements for a carrier-based light attack aircraft, the A-4 series attracted the interest of several friendly nations looking to upgrade their air defence capabilities. The Skyhawk's relatively low cost, high reliability and proven service with the US Navy and Marine Corps combined to make it a good buy for nations not involved in the development of their own aircraft. That interest offered the United States the advantages of keeping the Skyhawk production line in operation to meet current American needs while providing its allies with current-generation aircraft, establishing more weapons standardisation with its allies and, in some cases, developing a new use for refurbished A-4s replaced by newer models.

Argentina

Indeed, the first such overseas customer for the A-4 was the Republic of Argentina, which in 1965 concluded a $7.1 million agreement to acquire 50 refurbished A-4Bs for its air force (*Fuerza Aérea Argentina*). The aircraft came from US Navy surplus stocks and any necessary reworking was carried out at Douglas' plant in Tulsa, Oklahoma, where the first of the Argentine Air Force Skyhawks was flown on 31 December 1965. Redesignated A-4P, the initial batch of 25 aircraft was delivered in June 1966 and was followed by a second batch in 1970.

The Skyhawk's shipboard capability was not overlooked by naval authorities and, in 1971, the naval air arm (*Comando de Aviación Naval Argentina*) acquired 16 refurbished A-4B (redesignated A-4Q) aircraft. The two Argentine Skyhawk variants are virtually indistinguishable in appearance ; the primary differences are in some electronics equipment and in the engines, the A-4P being powered by the 7,700lb-thrust. J65-W-16A, the A-4Q by the 8,400lb thurst J65-W-20.

A-4G of VF-805 Squadron in the camouflage scheme sports unit insignia just aft of the air in-take

The naval Skyhawks were assigned to *3 Escuadrilla Aéronaval de Caza y Ataque* at the Commandante Espora naval air station, with elements of the unit deploying aboard Argentina's only aircraft carrier, the 695-foot-long, 16,000-ton *25 de Mayo* (ex-HMS *Venerable,* a World War II vintage British CVL, or light aircraft carrier).

The Argentine Air Force's continued interest in the Skyhawk was demonstrated in 1976, when it took delivery of 25 former A-4Cs that had been refurbished as A–4Qs. The Air Force Skyhawks have served with *I Escaudrón de Cazo Bombardiero* of *IV Brigada Aérea* at El Plumerillo air base in Mendoza and with *IV and V Escuadrones of V Brigada* at General Pringles air base at Villa Reynolds.

The plan for Argentine air power in the 1980s called for the Skyhawks to be replaced by Dassault-Bréguet Super Etendard supersonic figher aircraft. During the Falklands War of 1982, however, Argentine air force and naval Skyhawks played the most prominent role in their nation's efforts to win control of the disputed territory.

BBC television combat coverage and other illustrations subsequently released by the Ministry of Defence showed numerous instances of small, agile Skyhawks zooming perilously low over the water in their hard-driving efforts to cripple the strong Royal Navy force supporting the successful efforts to reinstate British control of the Falkland Islands. In fact, the Skyhawk was the most used Argentine aircraft of the 44-day conflict. Recently released information shows that of 'a total of 505 sorties from its continental bases . . . 149 (were undertaken) by A-4B Skyhawks, 106 by A-4C Skyhawks, 145 by IAI Daggers, 45 by Dassault-Bréguet Mirages, 54 by English Electric Canberras and six by IA-58 Pucaras.' The point is all the more interesting considering that '30 to 40 per cent (of the Skyhawks) were grounded by lack of spares – engines, drop tanks, ejection seat actuators, and so on – resulting from the embargo imposed on Argentina by the USA.'

Just as the US Navy deployed A-4s in Vietnam to undertake tough, precise ordnance delivery missions under heavy fire, the Argentine Skyhawks were assigned most of the anti-ship strike missions. Towards that end,

A line of A-4B aircraft converted to A-4P for export to the *Fuerza Aérea Argentina* (Argentine Air Force). the first 25 aircraft were in natural metal finish with national markings, as seen here. The semi-circular shadow seen on the fin is from the antenna for the modified electronic gear, a hallmark of all Argentine Skyhawks

ABOVE RIGHT
The second batch of A-4Ps provided to Argentina bore a camouflage scheme similar to that of the US Air Force, photographed here in California prior to delivery

RIGHT
One of the A-4Q aircraft provided to the *Comando de Aviación Naval Argentina* (Argentine Naval Air Arm) is readied for a test flight prior to delivery. The characteristic Argentine antenna is clearly visible on the fin, but the original A-4B Bureau Number (145053) is retained

they achieved recognized success. On 12 May, *Fuerza Aérea Argentina* Skyhawks attacked the destroyer HMS *Glasgow* and one of the A-4s succeeded in putting a 1,000lb bomb into the ship. However, the bomb kept right on going, and went out the other side without exploding. The Royal Navy, for its side, claimed to have shot down two of the A-4s, while a third crashed into the sea during evasive manoeuvres and a fourth was downed by friendly AAA fire.

On 25 May, Skyhawks were credited with sinking the destroyer HMS *Coventry*. However, the British claimed that defensive missiles hit five of the A-4s, including one flown Lieutenant R. Lucero, who ejected and became the only Argentine aviation prisoner until the surrender.

The distance they had to travel to the target area was a big drawback to A-4 operations in the Falklands. As the aircraft carrier *25 de Mayo* was out of service due to engine problems, all Skyhawk operations were carried out from bases in Argentina. Consequently, *FAA* A-4Bs at Rio Gallegos were 483 miles from Port Stanley in the Falklands and *Aviación Naval* A-4Qs and *FAA* A-4Cs at Rio Grande were 437 miles from the heart of the action. Thus, 'the 90 or so minutes occupied in flying to and from the operational area represented some 90 percent of the endurance of the aircraft, leaving scant time to seek out and attack targets'.

Adding to the Argentine Skyhawks' gauntlet of lack of state-of-the-art systems, lack of the operational flexibility of an aircraft carrier flight deck and the prospect of facing an array of new defensive missiles was the direct confrontation with highly-manoeuverable Harrier and Sea Harrier aircraft. In all other conflicts, conventional fighter cover had been enough to assure the A-4s security, but, in the Falklands fighting, the Royal Navy quickly recognized that the Argentine fighters remained largely at high altitude, leaving the low-altitude sphere to the A-4s – and the incredible performance of the 'jump jet fighters' from HMS *Invincible* and HMS *Hermes*.

The point is made abundantly clear in this account by the sole surviving A-4Q pilot from a sortie that left Rio Grande on the evening of 23 May:

'We found a frigate and attacked her with three aircraft. I saw the lead Skyhawk overfly the ship, launching a 500-lb bomb as the British launched a couple of missiles. These we evaded by violent jinking. I was now in a position to attack and dropped my bomb load which I saw

strike the enemy ship ; but Sea Harriers were now in hot pursuit behind us and my aircraft was soon struck by cannon fire. There were a lot of holes and many of my systems were inoperative, but I succeeded in evading the British fighters and headed for Puerto Argentino (Port Stanley) to attempt an emergency landing. I began my approach but found that I could not lower the undercarriage, so I ejected at 600 meters altitude. As I descended I saw that the pilotless Skyhawk was continuing to fly in circles, and it was later shot down by our own batteries'.

There has been no agreement on the casualties and victories of the Falklands War. The Argentine claim of '10 A-4B and eight A-4C Skyhawks . . . (with) two A-4Cs . . . known to have been so heavily damaged that they will not be repaired' is countered by the British claim of 45 A-4s 'shot down or probably destroyed'. Whatever they are, the A-4 losses don't accurately reflect the aircraft's performance in this unusual conflict. The distance, the poor Argentine logistics (for example, the two Lockheed KC-130H Hercules tankers available to support the entire effort) and, critically, the lack of a co-ordinated carrier air group all conspired against an otherwise strong combat aircraft.

Reliable reports indicate that a total of 24 ex-Israeli A-4E/H Skyhawks have been delivered to the *Aviación Naval* to make good wartime attrition, but these aircraft will probably be transferred to the *FAA* at a later date.

NAVY
903
NAVY
91

Two new build Australian Skyhawks are tested in California, an A-4G (left) and a TA-4G. Interestingly enough, the former bears a US-type Bureau Number (154903) on the aft of the fuselage

BELOW
VF-805 Squadron of the Royal Australian Navy has used two distinct colour schemes for its aircraft. Shown here aboard HMAS *Melbourne,* the forward A-4G bears the standard tail markings of the squadron whose nickname is the 'Checkmates'. The other aircraft bears the later camouflage scheme

Australia

After initial US Navy requirements for the TA-4E had been met in 1966, Douglas put the single-seat Skyhawk back into production to satisfy an Australian order for the eight A-4E and two TA-4E aircraft. The aircraft were to replace the Royal Australian Navy's older de Havilland Sea Venom FAW 53 jet fighters aboard the 16,000-ton HMAS *Melbourne* (ex-HMS *Majestic,* an unfinished World War II CVL subsequently completed to angle-deck configuration in 1955). Cost of the ten Skyhawks was £A 9 million. When completed, the aircraft were designated A-4G and TA-4G ; they were essentially A-4F and TA-4F types, with minor modifications to suit Australian requirements. First flights of the Australian Skyhawks were made on 19 July and 7 August 1967, respectively.

In 1971, eight refurbished US Navy A-4Fs and two TA-4Fs were provided to the RAN at a cost of £A 12 million. Interestingly enough, the 10 Skyhawks were picked up in San Diego, California and ferried back to Australia aboard HMAS *Sydney* (ex-HMS *Terrible,* an upgraded World War II CVL that subsequently became the RAN training carrier and then a transport ship). The single-seat Skyhawks were originally assigned to Australian fighter squadron VF-805, an historic unit dating back to World War II, which was recommissioned as an A-4G squadron in January 1968. In that unit, the Skyhawk's role was that of fighter bomber deployed aboard HMAS *Melbourne,* but unfortunately, nearly half the squadron's aircraft were lost due to operational accidents at sea. VF-805 was disbanded in 1982.

The two-seat Skyhawks were assigned to the training squadron VC-724 at Nowra, New South Wales. The dramatic (though hardly unexpected) decision of Bob Hawke, Australia's Prime Minister, to put *Melbourne* to the breaker's cutting torch has prompted a drastic re-organization of the RAN's Skyhawk force. Four of the carrier's A-4G Skyhawks are being retained as target tugs until June 1984. The other two A-4Gs will presumably remain in storage until terms are agreed with New Zealand for the sale of all six aircraft.

Indonesia

The reorganisation of Indonesian defence forces in 1974 resulted in a name-change for the air arm from the *Angkatan Udara Republik Indonesia* (AURI) to the *Tentara Nasional Indonesia - Angkatan Udara* (TNI-AU) or Indonesian Armed Forces - Air Force. The reorganisation and name-change were part of a significant shift in Indonesian foreign policy, from reliance on Soviet-built military supplies to those provided by the West. Consistent with that policy, in 1979 the Indonesian government applied for a stock of Skyhawks. The administration of President Carter served as broker in an arrangement under which the Indonesians would receive $25.8 million in financing for the purchase of 14 A-4E and two TA-4H aircraft from Israel. At that point Israel had purchased a total of 355 Skyhawks and was clearly interested in reducing its inventory of A-4Es acquired earlier in its defence programme. Moreover, the sale was consistent with the Israeli policy of refurbishing and selling its older aircraft to third world nations - usually with the approval of the nation that provided them to Israel. Hence, the US involvement in the Indonesian purchase. In late 1981, the Indonesian government announced plans to purchase 16 additional A-4E aircraft from US Navy surplus stocks. These aircraft, however, were to be supplied on an 'as is' basis, leaving to the buyer the matter of arranging refurbishing services. A $27 million price tag was placed on the deal.

A-4G of VF-805 Squadron taxies forward after landing on HMAS *Melbourne*

Israel

Israel acquired the greatest supply of export Skyhawks and, as noted, has become a source of reconditioned A-4s to other nations. Initially, Israel wanted to purchase a substantial quantity of refurbished A-4B aircraft. That offer, in 1965, was flatly refused by the US government. A year later, however, the Americans offered to sell Israel's neighbour Jordan a supply of ex-US Air Force Lockheed F-104C Starfighters. To help maintain the delicate balance of power in the Middle East, the US reopened the issue of an Israeli purchase of Skyhawks – and made the offer even more attractive by noting the availability of new aircraft. Consequently, 48 A-4F and two TA-4F aircraft were produced as A-4H and TA-4H aircraft for the Israeli Air Force (*Heyl Ha'Avir*).

The Skyhawk purchase was concluded at a most propitious time. After the Six Day War in 1967, France, Israel's leading supplier of combat aircraft, imposed an embargo on front-line aircraft slated for delivery to the *Heyl Ha'Avir*. Thus, it worked out well that the first Israeli Skyhawk made its maiden flight on 27 October 1967 and deliveries began soon thereafter. The A-4Hs were assigned the tactical attack role, in place of Dassault Mirage 5J aircraft affected by the embargo.

The A-4H differs from the US Navy version in that the Israeli aircraft were produced with enlarged and square-tipped vertical tail surfaces consistent with the use of a tail drogue braking parachute. The same feature was incorporated in subsequent new-build aircraft for export, as well as those subsequently provided to the US Marine Corps. The Israelis replaced the standard 20mm Mk 12 cannons in each wing root with their own version of the longer-barrel 30mm DEFA cannon; although the Mk 12 carried 200 rounds per gun – compared with 150 rpg for the DEFA weapon – the Israelis consider the cannon of their own manufacture to be more effective.

The first 50 Skyhawks were followed by a further shipment of 42 A-4Hs and ten TA-4Hs in 1969. That year, the *Heyl Ha'Avir* also began to receive the first examples of a consignment of 60 ex-US Navy A-4Es and 17 TA-4Js, delivery of the rest being spaced out over the next several years and into the period including the October 1973 war.

Tight Israeli security has made it extremely difficult to obtain in-depth information about the *Heyl Ha'Avir's* combat successes with the A-4. Routine information about individual pilots and squadrons is not provided (and photos of aircraft with squadron markings are censored) to keep Israel's hostile neighbours from learning too much about air operations. While there are reputed to be a number of air combat aces in the *Heyl Ha'Avir*, their indentities are masked to prevent reprisals against their families by anti-Israeli terrorists.

Despite these restrictions, the Skyhawk's value can be seen in a report published some time after the Six Day

RESCUE
885

Approaching to land at a shore base, this A-4G of VF-805 Squadron bears the unit insignia on the fin. Commissioned as No. 805 Squadron RAAF, in Egypt in 1940, the unit still retains a palm tree design in its insignia – unusual for a naval unit, but it does reflect its history

89

NAVY
880
N-13 154911

LEFT
Australian Skyhawks perform the same functions as their US counterparts and, as in this case, use the same refuelling equipment and other stores

BELOW
TA-4G of VF-805 ready for take-off from Nowra, New South Wales, the airfield is also used by VC-724

War. At that time, the *Heyl Ha'Avir* was beginning to recieve A-4Es, all of which were assigned to one base, while the A-4Hs were assigned to squadrons at another.

At the A-4E base, an Israeli source noted: 'The Skyhawk was given a thorough shake-down on operations before the cease-fire of August last year (1970), and although the pilot of a MiG-21MF or other high-performance Soviet fighter now being flown by the Egyptians can undoubtedly break off combat with our aircraft at will, we have no doubt that our Skyhawks, with their outstanding manoeuvrability, are fully capable of defending themselves. Prior to the cease-fire, one of our Skyhawks had downed a Syrian MiG-19 over Lebanon with a 2.5in (6.35cm) air-to-ground rocket! Another had bagged a MiG-17 with its DEFA cannon.

The A-4 in any version was not intended to be a fighter aircraft and, indeed, Israeli Skyhawks did not usually engage enemy aircraft unless attacked. The big advantage of the A-4H over its French-built predecessors was in its ability to deliver twice the ordnance to a given target : an 8,200lb ordnance load for the A-4H as compared to a 4,000lb load for the Dassault Mirage IIIC used during the Six Day War.

The unsettling events prior to the 1970 cease-fire gave the Israelis an opportunity to learn, as had the Americans during the Vietnam War, just how rugged the Skyhawk is. An example cited is the A-4E heading home from a deep penetration of Egytian territory on 29 July 1970. The ex-US Navy Skyhawk was attacked by a much superior MiG-21MF (Fishbed-J), which fired an Atoll air-to-air missile at the Israeli aircraft. The missile hit the Skyhawk punctured the wing, but the A-4 was able to elude its pursuer and return to its base.

That incident was part of a large action in which MiG-21s had driven back a comparatively small force of Skyhawks and Mirage IIICs. The following day the Israelis settled the score by sending a similar small force in the direction of Inchas, an Egyptian base believed to have been manned by Soviet advisors and pilots. When the Fishbed-J fighters rose to the bait, a sizeable force of Israeli Phantom and Mirage jet fighters met the MiGs at the border, south of the city of Suez, and closed in on them. The damaged Skyhawk of the day before was avenged by the destruction of four of the MiGs. The Israelis suffered no losses that day.

Israel has acknowledged some Skyhawk casualties due to events prior to the 8 August 1970 cease-fire. Most of those losses, however, were caused by Soviet-built SA-2 surface-to-air missiles (SAMs). Consequently, the avionics package developed during the Vietnam War for US Navy A-4F aircraft was quickly acquired by the *Heyl Ha'Avir* and fitted to its A-4E and A-4H aircraft.

During the 18-day Yom Kippur War of October 1973, Israeli losses were considerably higher, with a total of 104 aircraft confirmed as lost. There is no official break-down of those losses, but 53 Skyhawks were assumed to be among them. Subsequently, the Israeli government applied for some $2,000 million worth of American-made armaments including 'a large proportion' of Phantom and Skyhawk jet aircraft.

Beginning in late 1972, the Israelis also took delivery of its first A-4N aircraft. Based on the A-4M developed for the US Marine Corps, the 117 A-4Ns ordered by Israel have an improved navigational attack system and revised cockpit design. A number of A-4Ns have been modified so the tailpipe is extended further aft to 'push' heat emission farther behind the aircraft, thus counteracting the effectiveness of the new Soviet-built SA-7 SAMs being supplied to nations hostile to Israel. The A-4N is referred to as the Skyhawk II.

Skyhawks have served the *Heyl Ha'Avir* well and, despite a planned reduction of numbers through overseas sales, A-4s should continue in front-line Israeli operations through much of the 1980s.

Kuwait

In the Persian Gulf, where radical governments have begun to appear too frequently to suit pro-Western or neutral leaders in the area, security is often measured by supplies of modern weaponry. Thus, when the State of Kuwait began routinely upgrading its defence inventory in the early 1970s, the later model A-4 aircraft looked highly attractive.

Consequently, on 7 November 1974, the Kuwaiti government signed a contract to purchase 36 new-build A-4M aircraft. The $250 million cost included spares, support equipment and the training of Kuwait Air Force personnel. Initially it was felt that the KAF would add both SEPECAT Jaguar International *and* McDonnell Douglas A-4M aircraft, but it was eventually revealed that the cost-effective Skyhawk had won another contest on its basic virtue of comparatively low and stable acquisition cost. BAC, co-producers of the Anglo-French strike aircraft, were reluctant to supply a long-lead contract without escalation clauses, while McDonnell Douglas were able to offer a fixed-price contract with completion of A-4M deliveries in 1976.

The Skyhawk purchase was explained as being part of a long-term Kuwaiti armed forces expansion programme costing $1,000 million and including at least the potential basing of KAF elements in Abu Dhabi, Bahrain and Qatar. As a first step, within a year of signing the Skyhawk contract, the Kuwaitis began work on two additional air bases south and west of the KAF's single airfield.

Designated the A-4KU, the first of the Kuwaiti Skyhawks flew on 20 July 1976, followed by the first TA-4KU on 14 December. Eventually, the KAF received 30 single-seater and six two-seat trainers.

In the opinion of one highly knowledgeable source, the Kuwait Air Force may well have had 'the best of the Skyhawks.' That praise came from Douglas production

NAVY

Flightdeck crewmen aboard HMAS *Melbourne* secure an A-4G of VF-805 Squadron after flight operations

test pilot Jim Stegman. A former Marine Corps pilot, Stegman joined Douglas in 1955, just in time to begin test flying each Skyhawk that rolled off the Douglas El Segundo production line. He was assisted by other pilots in peak production periods during the Vietnam War, but otherwise Jim Stegman has flown most of the A-4s in the World today. His log book shows well over 3,000 hours in A-4s, including extensive manoeuvres over the southern California desert.

Stegman usually flew each Skyhawk two or three times, performing components of every types of mission. 'I've never had to get out of one,' he said prior to his retirement from Douglas after the A-4 went out of production, 'but I've had just about every other kind of emergency there is.'

When asked in 1977 which Skyhawk model was his favourite, he immediately said it was the A-4KU. 'With that P-408A engine, she's really a rocket – a sweetheart.'

Stegman's reference was to the 11,200lb-thrust Pratt & Whitney J52-P-408A engine, the most powerful in the line of Skyhawk power-plants, which was first used in the A-4M and then on all subsequent new-build aircraft.

ABOVE
An A-4H of the Israeli Air Force *Heyl Ha'Avir* returns from a bombing mission. The *Heyl Ha'Avir* has operated A-4E, A-4H and A-4N all later being modified in Israel to Skyhawk II standard by fitting the dorsal avionics pack, drag parachute and square tip fin. All models are fitted with the 30mm DEFA cannon

RIGHT
A-4's of the *Heyl Ha'Avir* are painted in a unique three colour camouflage scheme. The Israeli censor has removed, from these photographs, both the squadron badge and aircraft number

New-build A-4H for Israel's *Heyl Ha'Avir* bears US markings while being test flown by Douglas. US-type Bureau Number (155254) simply keeps production sequence in order

254
A-4H
155254 A

RESCUE
DANGER
726

LEFT
Israeli A-4N, similarity to the US Marine Corps' A-4M, reflects the high state of development of the last Skyhawks produced. The chin blister houses sophisticated electronic counter measures equipment (ECM)

ABOVE
Intended solely for export, the A-4N was christened the 'Skyhawk II'. In Israeli service, the A-4N sports two 30-mm DEFA cannons, new navigation/weapons delivery system and a revised cockpit lay-out. It also used standard US weapons such as the AGM-12 Bullpup air-to-ground missile from outboard ordnance stations

ABOVE
Although not a carrier-based aircraft, the A-4N retains the Navy-type tailhook for use with mobile arresting gear (MOREST)

RIGHT
Prior to delivery, this TA-4KU bore US markings and had an instrument sensor fitted to the refuelling probe

BELOW
Considered by many Skyhawk pilots to be the finest of the series, the Kuwait Air Force A-4KU aircraft are equipped with the powerful Pratt & Whitney 11,200-lb thrust J52-P-408A engine and the latest avionics equipment

Malaysia

Following protracted negotiations, the Malaysian Government has signed with Grumman Aerospace for 40 ex-US Navy Skyhawks, including six TA-4 trainers.

New Zealand

In 1970, the Royal New Zealand Air Force (RNZAF) took delivery of the first of ten single-seat and four two-seat Skyhawks designated A-4K and TA-4K, respectively. The New Zealand aircraft were based on the A-4F and TA-4F production models, but with modifications found in the A-4H and A-4M aircraft (braking drogue parachutes, attendant fin design change and modified radios).

The new aircraft replaced the RNZAF's ageing de Havilland Vampire FB5 and T11 aircraft and were assigned to 14 Squadron for operational conversion duties and to 75 Squadron for fulfillment of several missions. With the retirement of the RNZAF's obsolescent English Electric B(1)12 and T13 Canberra light bombers, the A-4Ks quickly became New Zealand's front-line strike force. The A-4Ks fly close air support, interdiction, anti-shipping, limited air defence and coastal surveillance. In addition to missions flown in and around New Zealand, 75 Squadron's Skyhawks participate in joint exercises throughout the South Pacific, as current Air Staff policy calls for overseas tours on a three-year cycle. Thus, the unit may make a tour to Australia one year, the United States (usually the western outpost of Hawaii) the next and exercise with one or more south-east asian neighbours (Singapore, Malaysia and Indonesia) the next.

Despite a heavy operational schedule, to date, only one of the 14 aircraft has been lost. In that instance, the results of an investigation showed that the A-4K crash at Ohakea on 18 October 1974 was due to oil pump failure. The pump had been incorrectly assembled and when it ceased functioning, caused complete engine failure. The RNZAF were planning to acquire a replacement aircraft, possibly an ex-US Navy Skyhawk with low flight time on it.

The anti-shipping role, particulary important to an island nation, is described by Ross Ewing, one of the first 10 RNZAF pilots to convert to the aircraft:

'In the anti-shipping role, the Skyhawk is in its element ; even in today's age of surface-to-air-missile (SAM) accuracy and availability, the low, low-flying Skyhawk over water presents a formidable opponent. With a frontal surface area of not much more than the underside of a large car, the A-4 provides a very small radar target, and at 50 feet (or less) above the waves the earth's curvature prevents detection by ship-borne radar until it is literally there. But over land, recent trends in tactics observed overseas (Vietnam and Middle East) where the A-4s have been in service, have lead to a move away from the low-level strikes of World War II fame to high-speed, medium-level mass attacks (SAMs are more easily out-manoeuvred at medium level – 10,000 to 15,000 feet – and also get confused by large numbers of aircraft), although in the most recent Middle East conflict more numbers than ever before of Israeli A-4s were lost in intial battles, mainly due to SAMs. Future strategies possibly surround advances in electronic wizardry which could be fitted to aircraft to outsmart the SAM homing devices. The RNZAF's A-4s currently have no ECM gear fitted to the hump, but the space is there for such a fit.'

The RNZAF will no doubt continue to use A-4Ks to meet ANZUS Treaty and their own defence requirements for some years to come. The acquisition of Australia's six surplus A-4Gs should stretch the operational life of the RNZAF's existing fleet into the 1990s.

RIGHT
Wings and forward fuselage sections are transported from Douglas' Long Beach plant to Palmdale, where they will be mated to tail sections and fitted with the electronics equipment usually acquired directly by the ordering government

BELOW
Near the end of the Skyhawk production, a small scale line was maintained. Here, A-4KU cockpits are first assembled, painted black and then pressure checked for leaks. In the production process it has taken about six months to reach this point

Sierracin

A-4KU
160190A

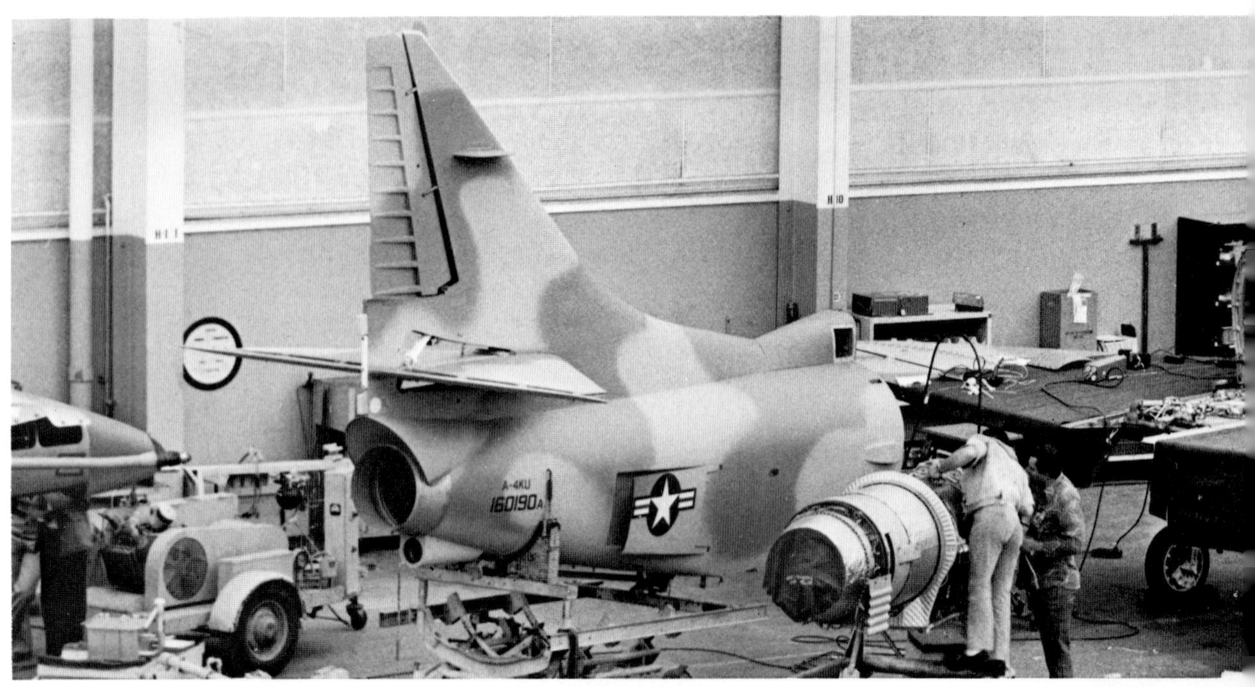

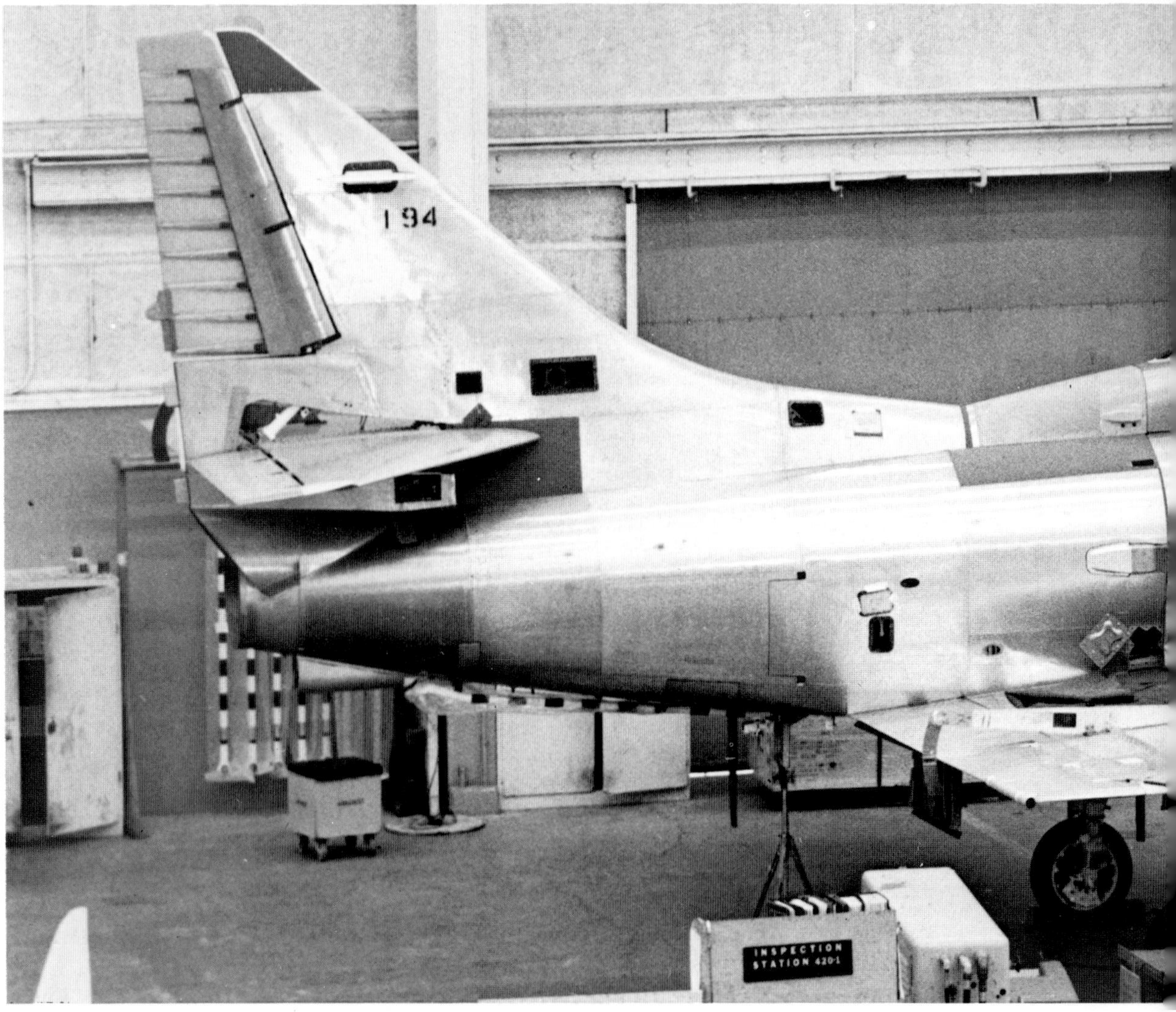
194
INSPECTION
STATION 420-1

LEFT
At the final assembly point, the A-4KU is painted and the engine is installed. A number of ground tests follow and after the aircraft is flown extensively prior to delivery

BELOW
A nearly completed A-4KU has its variety of electronic equipment installed and then moves to the end of the production line

Singapore

In 1972 the Republic of Singapore announced the purchase of 40 refurbished ex-US Navy A-4B aircraft for its Air Defence Command (SADC). It was a dramatic move for the young independent service, which only three years earlier had acquired its first aircraft (nine Cessna 172Ks for primary training), but it was part of a quick catch-up by the SADC, which had already added 20 Hawker Hunters in 1970 to assure that it played a meaningful role in air defence of the area.

The A-4B refurbishing contract was awarded to Lockheed Aircraft Service Company (LAS), a division of Lockheed Corporation with experience in aircraft modification and maintenance dating back to 1938. From its headquarters in Ontario, California, LAS operates domestic and international bases to serve its US and foreign customers. In the case of the SADC contract, an intial batch of eight A-4Bs was transported from the US government's surplus aircraft storage facility at Davis-Monthan Air Force Base, Arizona, to the LAS facility in California.

The programme included a complete inspection and repair to the airframes, as well as several major modifications : installation of solid-state electronics for communications, new radio and navigation-attack systems including a Ferranti ISIS D-101 lead-computing gunsight, redesigned cockpit to accommodate new instrumentation and control boxes, spoilers and a braking parachute. Although not intended for carrier-based flight operations, the aircraft retained the arrester hook for Short Airfield for Tactical Support (SATS) operation. The refurbished aircraft, given the designation A-4S, were similar to the new-build A-4Ms, except that there was no provision for using Bullpup missiles, two 30mm Mk 4 Aden cannons were fitted in the wing roots and the 8,100lb-thrust J65-W-20 engine was installed. Likewise, most of the electronic equipment, housed in a slightly longer nose, was of British origin to enhance the servicing compatibility with the SADC's Hunters.

LAS also provided maintenance and pilot training equipment and support in addition to a logistics support programme. In the spring of 1974, the first six SADC pilots completed a 20-week advanced jet training syllabus in TA-4J aircraft at NAS Chase Field, Texas. They then went on to single-seat A-4 training with Readiness Air Group 12 at NAS Lemoore, California. During the following two years, 42 additional SADC pilots went through the same training to complete Singapore's requirements for a supply of Skyhawk-qualified pilots. In turn, a number of those pilots established a Singapore-based training programme.

In anticipation of the local training and maintenance effort, Lockheed Aircraft Service Company completed remanufacture of the remaining 32 A-4s at its facility in Singapore. LAS also produced the most distinctive-looking two-seat Skyhawk trainer of the series. Designated TA-4S and first flown on 14 July 1973, the Singapore two-seater was manufactured from components of two basic A-4Bs, giving the aircraft the expanded capability of a second pilot or mission commander if the aircraft had to augment its training role by being used in combat. Thus, rather than using the longer canopy of regular TA-4 aircraft, the TA-4S has separate tandem cockpits, each with its own canopy. The SADC ordered only seven TA-4S aircraft and, rather than having to stock a limited number of TA-4 replacement canopies, it elected to use the tandem arrangement, so that any needed replacements could come from normal stores. The SADC thereby saved money in both manufacturing and logistics.

The A-4S Skyhawks were assigned to 142 Gryphon and 143 Phoenix Squadrons at Tenagh. However, some examples also serve with 141 Squadron, which had used Hunters exclusively. A long-term maintenance programme has been established for the A-4S and TA-4S aircraft, leading to the conclusion that both aircraft will be in service through the 1980s and possibly beyond.

Veteran Douglas test pilot Jim Stegman has flown over 7,000 hours in more different individual A-4s than any other pilot

ABOVE RIGHT
A new A-4K and a new TA-4K built for the Royal New Zealand Air Force go through their paces in California prior to delivery

RIGHT
When the RNZAF A-4K Skyhawks reach their destination, the insignia of No.75 Squadron is applied just aft of the intake. One of the RNZAF roles is maritime strike

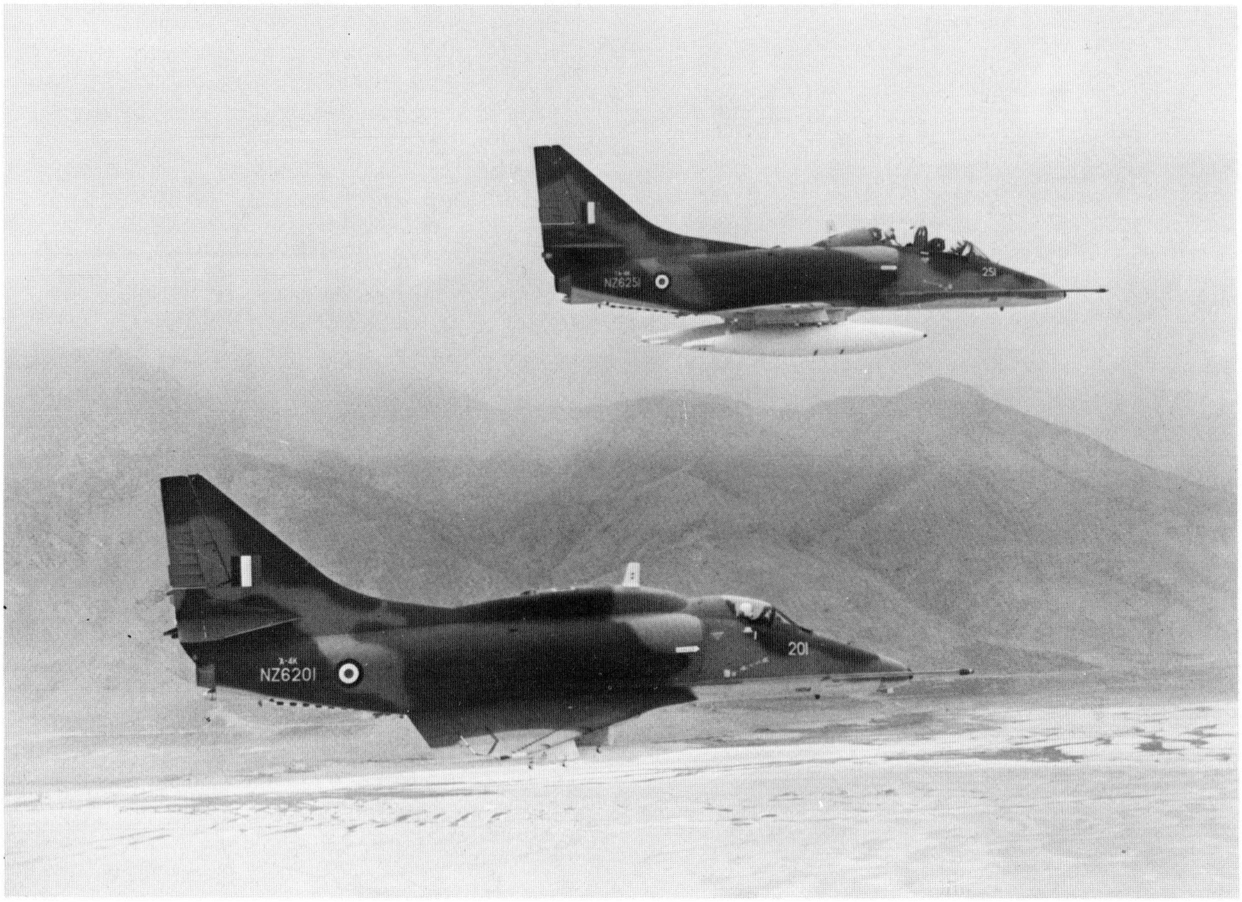
NZ6251
251
A-4K
NZ6201
201

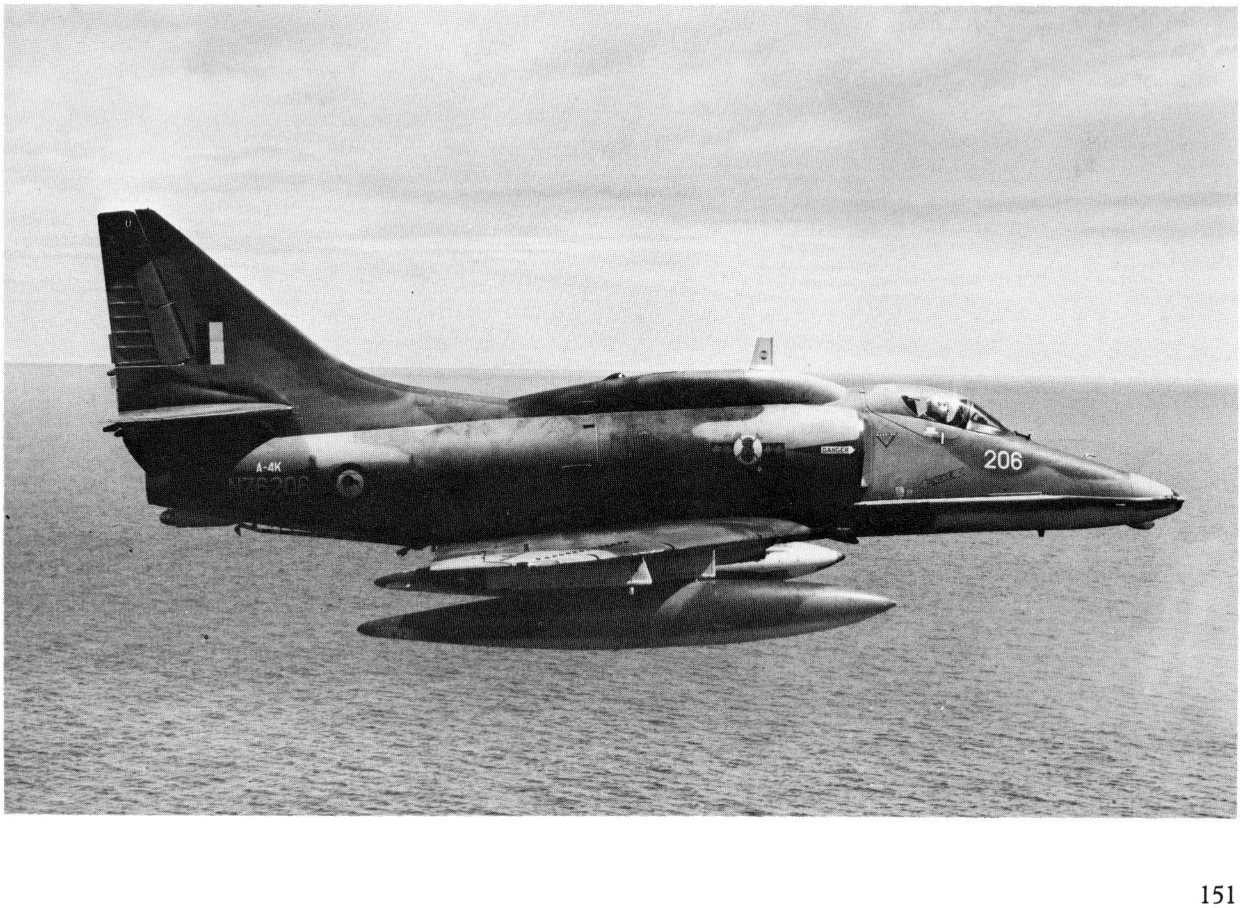
A-4K
DANGER
206

A trio of RNZAF A-4Ks practice close-formation flying over the New Zealand countryside

DANGER

A-4S
602
02

ABOVE
The third A-4S in flight over California during training of the Singapore pilots

ABOVE LEFT
The third A-4S conversion for the Singapore Air Defence Command, an ex-Navy A-4B reworked by Lockheed Aircraft Service Company in Ontario, California. A noticeable feature is the angled refuelling probe, unlike the straight type found on original A-4B aircraft

LEFT
The first eight A-4S Skyhawks to be modified by Lockheed Aircraft Service Company in Ontario, California lined up at NAS Lemoore for use in the Republic of Singapore pilot training programme during 1974

Other Foreign Efforts

A number of foreign countries have indicated an interest in acquiring either new-build A-4s or ex-service examples. At one point, for example, Malaysia intended to purchase some 88 ex-US Navy A-4C and A-4L aircraft but finally decided on a total buy of 40 A-4s. Prior to its near collapse of recent years, the government of Lebanon had also shown interest in the Skyhawk and, given a degree of success by current efforts at national unity, the Lebanese may yet acquire a supply from neighbouring Israel.

One of the most intriguing overseas offers was made in the mid 1960s, when a foreign-engined variant was offered to European nations on a co-production basis. In 1965, Douglas competed against LTV and Northrop for a major Canadian contract by offering a single-seat CA-4E and two-seat CA-4F aircraft to meet the requirement for a new light-weight fighter-attack aircraft. Aside from minor design changes, which would have given the Canadian version a long, but lower two-place canopy, the CA-4 would have been powered by the 12,000lb-thrust Rolls-Royce RB168-20 Spey turbofan engine. Compared to the LTV A-7A and Northrop F-5A, the Spey A-4 would have been a bargain at $764,000.

The Spey A-4 was not purchased by the Canadians, but Douglas went straight to work on US allies in NATO and offered it as proposed new equipment for the reconnaissance, strike and close air support role requirements of Belgium, Holland and Italy. That proposal was not accepted, but it did not mean the end of European interest in the A-4.

On 18 September 1972, two A-4Ms flown by pilots from the US Naval Air Test Center at Patuxent River, Maryland, began suitability demonstrations aboard the French aircraft carrier *Foch*. The French *Aéronavale* was looking for a replacement for its Dassault Etendard IVM and IVP light-weight strike and reconnaissance aircraft. One important factor, of course, was the proposed replacement's ability to operate from the relatively short flight-decks of the 845ft-long 31,000-ton carriers *Foch* and *Clémenceau*. Neither deck was much shorter than those of the *Essex*-class carriers on which the A-4 had first been deployed and which served among their sea-going bases during the Vietnam War. Hence, the A-4 was a natural contender to succeed the Etendard naval aircraft.

The carrier suitability tests were soon called off, however, when it was realised that catapult track covers on the French ships would not support the Skyhawk's nosewheel. The problem could have been overcome by lengthening and strengthening the catapults on both French carriers, which would have enhanced their ability to operate other naval aircraft, but the A-4 was not selected – probably for political rather than operational reasons. The *Aéronavale* was already operating American-built LTV F-8E(FN) Crusader supersonic fighters and going overseas for yet another ship-based aircraft to serve in France's two-carrier navy was probably more than the delicate national ego would tolerate. Consequently, the considerably more expensive Dassault-Bréguet Super Etendard development of the original IVM eventually entered French naval aviation service.

There will most likely be additional foreign users of the A-4 series. As the principal holders of A-4s – the US Navy and Israel's Air Force – remove their first-line Skyhawks from service, these aircraft (including many later models) became an affordable resource to a number of smaller, friendly nations. It is a resource that will surely be used for years to come.

The TA-4S, made from components of two A-4Bs, was delivered in the new national and standard camouflage markings of the Singapore Air Defence Command. The dorsal avionics fairing, however, remained black

RIGHT
An early test flight of the first TA-4S conversion was undertaken when the aircraft had only a natural metal finish

6
Skyhawks Forever

When the last Skyhawk, A-4M BuNo 160264, was delivered to the Fleet it became a noteworthy event in American aviation history. Accordingly, on 27 February 1979, McDonnell Douglas Corporation arranged a suitable final roll-out ceremony. Douglas Aircraft Company president John C. Brizendine and Ed Heinemann, retired by that time, presented that last A-4's logbooks to Captain E. W. Melvin, the Navy plant representative at Douglas. Captain Melvin accepted the aircraft for the Navy and then turned the logbooks over to Lieutenant Colonel M. R. (Sid) Snedecker, commanding officer of VMA-331.

In reporting that event, the quarterly magazine of The Tailhook Association voiced a sentiment shared by many A-4 aficionados, hoping that the ceremony would become an annual event for several years to come – The Last Skyhawk Rollout. 'It just doesn't seem possible that after 27 years there won't be any more Skyhawks built. This feisty little airplane has become such a part of naval aviation like none other before it and in a variety of roles that were never dreamed of during its design, that it is unacceptable to say "no more".

'On several occasions during the long history of the Skyhawk, it seemed that production of the durable jet would end,' the article continued, 'but each time the defence requirement for ruggedness, versatility, performance and low cost dictated additional orders. Key to the long life of the Skyhawk was the McDonnell Douglas-Navy program of continuing improvement with more powerful engines, advanced navigation and weapons delivery systems and more armament capability.

'At one point in its career, Navy personnel were so proud of the Skyhawk's survivability *(sic)* – both in combat and as a production program – that they distributed bumper stickers reading "A-4s Forever".

A close head-on pass by two Skyhawks demonstrates not only the pilots skill in coordinated flying, but also their ability to manouevre in one-on-one situations, such as aerial combat

'And, while the squadrons of Skyhawks in operation in the US and overseas will not last forever, many of them will still be soaring through the skies into the beginning of the 21st century.'

While the last roll-out ceremony at El Segundo did, in fact, mark delivery of the 2,960th – and last – production Skyhawk, the final prediction of the magazine article will most surely come true. The A-4 Skyhawk series could well become to light attack, close air support and training roles what the venerable Douglas DC-3 has become to the civilian air transport industry, within which many small carriers continue to operate the 'gooney bird' nearly 50 years after its first roll-out.

Training Command

In the US Navy Training Comman, which qualifies Navy and Marine Corps officers for subsequent assignment to Fleet squadrons, the TA-4J has replaced the Grumman TA-9J Cougar as the advanced fighter and attack training aircraft. The TA-4 began operations with training squadrons VT-21 and VT-22 at NAS Kingsville, Texas, in 1969. Since then, TA-4s have been supplied to all Navy advanced training units.

In the current training syllabus, student pilots receive basic flight training in the North American Rockwell T-2 Buckeye and then move up to the two-seat Skyhawk. Flying the TA-4J is an exciting experience that is endearing the Skyhawk to a whole new generation of naval aviators, as noted by Marine Corps First Lieutenant James Swofford, a two-year veteran of the Training Command. He has flown the North American Rockwell T-28 Trojan, the T-2 (in which he is presently an instructor) and the TA-4. The latter is clearly his favourite:

'It's a big step forward to go from the T-2C syllabus for intermediate jets to the TA-4J. At that point, you're a fairly good pilot, knowning the basics of instruments, formation flying and carrier landings. All you lack is tactical training, which is a good portion of the Advanced Strike Syllabus in the TA-4J. Once you have that

501
RESCUE

TOP
The first TA-4E (BuNo 152102), subsequently a TA-4F and then converted to a TA-4J over the long and continuing life of the two-seat Skyhawk

ABOVE
A brand-new A-4F, with a straight test instruments probe, in place of the refuelling equipment, taxies out from the Douglas flight test line

LEFT
The Skyhawk was in the Vietnam War right to the bitter end. Here, Commander Almer C. Vould, commanding officer of the 'Warhorses' VA-55, flies a practice mission in an A-4F over California prior to the squadron's last deployment aboard USS *Hancock* (CVA-19) from March to October 1975. On this seventh and final cruise in support of operations in Indo-China, VA-55 was on hand during the evacuation of American and allied personnel from South Vietnam and Cambodia. It was also the last cruise for USS *Hancock*, a veteran of World War II and 17 post-war cruises to the Western Pacific. After carrier air wing CVW-21 disembarked in 1975, the *Essex*-class carrier was decommissioned and subsequently sold for scrap

NAVY

experience, you feel confident that you can fly whatever Fleet aircraft are involved in your first permanent squadron assignment.

'Initially, you fly in the back seat of the TA-4J while practising for your instrument ticket which qualifies you to fly in the airways. That's important in accomplishing advanced syllabus flights of related aircraft in the Fleet, involving mostly solo flights in all weather conditions.

'With instrument training out of the way, you graduate to the front seat, and that's when the fun begins. That's when you really feel it's your aircraft. Unlike the T-2C, with engines slung beneath the centreline, the TA-4J has its thrust on centreline and requires fewer attitude adjustments from the pilot. This is a nice feature for the new guy who has his hands full. the TA-4J goes where you point it, faster or slower ; it does not pitch up or down with power movements, as the T-2C does.

LEFT
A pair of unmarked TA-4F Skyhawks prior to initial flights with test instrument probes

'The TA-4J *is* generally flown about 50 knots faster than the T-2C and averages 25 knots faster in the landing pattern. Coming in on "the ball" (line-up point for the mirror landing system aboard an aircraft carrier) is a lot tougher in the TA-4J as the higher approach speed leaves less room for error. The TA-4J teaches you to think quicker and anticipate events sooner. The CQ (carrier qualification) stage is, therefore, more demanding. Inattention during CQ's *could* cause you to drop in low, resulting in a "hook slap" (arresting hook striking the flight deck before it engages the wire), and the student aviators Landing Signal Officer (LSO) will quickly send you home for that. Better performance is demanded by this stage.

'Since the TA-4J *is* less forgiving than the T-2C, one has to be sharper in every aspect of flying. The TA-4J engine, less powerful than the TA-4F's, doesn't respond as fast in the landing pattern as the twin-engines of the T-2C.

BELOW
The two-seat Skyhawk has good bomb and missile capabilities, even though the TA-4J has a less powerful engine

124

LEFT
A TA-4J of the US Navy's Training Command approaches to land aboard the training carrier USS *Lexington* (CVT-16), in the Gulf of Mexico

TOP
TA-4J of training squadron VT-21 shows the forward retracting undercarriage as it departs from NAS Kingsville, Texas

ABOVE
From above a TA-4J of VT-21 shows the large day-glo orange panels that make these training aircraft easily visible

It doesn't usually happen, but should you ever become low on "the ball" and slow – about 17½ units AOA (angle of attack) – and back on the power, there will be a lag after power addition before the power takes effect ; but if you think ahead, you won't have that kind of a problem.'

There are, of course, incidents for which a pilot cannot plan and, as Lieutenant Swofford recalls, those are the times when the aircraft's basic reliability is the key to a safe return to base.

'One time we were flying a weapons pattern, circling at about 8,000 feet. You usually come in, dive on a target, get all of your parameters straight (airspeed, dive angle, etc), release your bomb, pull-off and come around again for another try. There are usually four airplanes doing this at any one time, so it is a fairly fast-past pattern.

'Upon reaching the run-in line, I pulled right, rolled inverted, lowered my nose to my dive angle and rolled out. I made my delivery, but, during my 4g pull-off, I suddenly began to stream fuel. One of the other pilots said I was on fire, but a visual check of all I could see of the aircraft and a look at all my gauges didn't reveal anything unusual. So I made another dive, but when I pulled up, I was again told I had lost a lot of fuel. I noticed a slight drop in my fuel gauge.

'The instructor came out of the pattern to take a good look at my airplane. He didn't see anything wrong and told me to continue. The next dive was fine, but after the pull-off I was streaming fuel continuously. The fuel gauge was going down as I watched it, so I turned immediately for the airfield.

'As soon as I started my emergency descent, the fuel leak stopped and I made an uneventful landing. There was no fuel leak once I was on the ground, so I taxied back to the flight line and got another plane and was soon finishing my "hop" that afternoon. They fixed the first plane that night and discovered that a sticky fuel valve had caused the problem. Minor emergencies such this test students' abilities, but the good, solid TA-4J rarely makes a student walk home.'

Air Combat Manoeuvring

While never intended to be a fighter aircraft, the fast and manoeuvrable A-4 serves as an enemy fighter surrogate in the US Navy's dedicated effort to sharpen the dogfighting skills of it's fighter pilots. A bitter lesson of the early days of the Vietnam War was that fast, sophisticated fighters with modern weapons *still* needed the basic elements of aerial dogfighting to be successful. On too many occasions, chronologically inferior North Vietnamese fighters – MiG-17s and -19s – were bringing down state-of-the-art American fighter aircraft.

LEFT
Day-glo orange panels on the bottom wing surfaces, of this TA-4J, show clearly as it banks away from the camera aircraft

First Lieutenant James Swofford, a US Marine Corps training instructor at NAS Kingsville, sits atop his mount a TA-4J

That realisation brought about the establishment of air combat manoeuvring (ACM) as a point of emphasis in fighter training. The small, manoeuvrable A-4 offered many of the characteristics of the older Soviet-built aircraft being supplied to North Vietnam and therefore became an ideal adversary aircraft to teach Navy fighter pilots to out-manoeuvre their opponents and *then* bring to bear the sophisticated weapons systems that highlighted American aircraft superiority.

The success of the programme is seen in this example noted by Lieutenant Commander Tom (Killer) Kilcline, an A-4 pilot with VF-126, the Pacific Fleet adversary squadron, stationed at NAS Miramar, California :

'Boring in on the enemy aircraft, the F-4 pilot noticed the MiG-17's nose light up. He immediately pulled hard into the vertical as he realized this guy was firing 23mm . . . wait a minute, the A-4s he had fought against during his training had never shot back ! To his amazement the MiG zoomed with him and there he was straight up, canopy to canopy, not more than 30 feet away from his adversary. He outzoomed the MiG but as he went over the top he made a predictable move and the wiley MiG pilot quickly took advantage.

'With the tracers passing close aboard, the F-4 rolled out straight down with the MiG right behind. Not willing to admit the "Gomer" could be that good, he told his RIO (radar intercept officer), "All right, we'll get this guy now". As the MiG's nose committed down, the F-4 pilot pulled into him and began a rolling scissors. The MiG went nose high and suddenly the Navy jock remembered his training against the A-4 . . . months earlier, when fighting against a VF-126 A-4E piloted by VF-121's Lieutenant Dave Frost, he had seen the same move. He knew he could run out using gravity to his advantage and gain a mile to a mile-and-a half out of range before the MiG would be nose on again. It worked! He now could turn and re-engage. After several more rolling scissors, he finally split the MiG out in front and fired a Sidewinder, which quickly ended the contest of pilot skills.

'This engagement ended with Lieutenant Randy Cunningham's and Lieutenant (junior grade) Willie Driscoll's fifth kill and their opponent's first loss after 13 victories ; he was the North Vietnamese Air Force's leading ace, Colonel Tomb. It was also significant because it graphically demonstrated the worth of realistic adversary training when engaged in actual combat.'

TA-4Js of Marine attack training squadron VMAT-102 give the advance students first-hand experience in firing air-to-surface weapons

MARINES

ABOVE
Acting as the aggressor in an Air Combat Maneuovring (ACM) exercise, Commander Rod Knutson, commanding officer of VF-126, 'patrols' the skies of Southern California in a blue and grey A-4F with Soviet-type identification numerals on the forward fuselage

RIGHT
Once the 'battle' begins, Commander Knutson turns into his adversary, a Grumman F-14A of the 'Sundowners' VF-111. The smaller, nimble Skyhawk gives the 'fighter jocks' plenty to think about during ACM exercises

TOP
Giving the initial impression of a lengthened-fuselage, four-man Skyhawk, this view examplifies the team's skill and coordination

ABOVE
The US Navy 'Blue Angels' flight demonstration team fly their navy blue and gold A-4Fs (minus the avionics package) at air shows throughout the US to demonstrate the high level of flight proficiency possible with a first-rate aircraft in the hands of top pilots. The 1982-83 team, seen here, is composed of (from left): Lieutenant Bud Hunsucker, Lieutenant Randy Clark, Lieutenant Commander Bob Stephens, Marine Corps Major Jim Dineen, Commander Dave Carroll (commanding officer), Lieutenant Kevin Miller, Lieutenant Commander Stu Powrie, and Lieutenant Scott Anderson

RIGHT
Six A-4F's of the 'Blue Angels' on a practice flight over California

5
U.S.NAVY
Blue Angels
2
U.S.NAVY
3
U.S.NAVY
Blue Angels
1
U.S.NAVY
Blue Angels

The Pacific Fleet's ACM squadron has a long association with the A-4 series. Originally designated VA-126, the unit operated F7U-3 Cutlass and later F9F-8B Cougar and FJ-4B Fury fighters before it became affected by the establishment of Fleet Replacement Air Groups (RAGs) in late 1959. At that point, VA-126 combined with elements of VF-54 and VA-125 to become a RAG for the A4D-1 Skyhawk, as well as the AD-5, -6 and -7 variants of the Skyraider. In 1960, VA-126 assumed the light attack training role, using the F9F-8T, the available two-seater at the time, for instrument training. The squadron was redesignated VF-126 in October 1965, but maintained its affiliation with attack aircraft and transitioned to the TA-4F in April 1967.

To meet the need for additional fighter pilot training in ACM, the Navy Fighter Weapons School (abbreviated NFWS, but better known as 'Top Gun') was established in January 1972, with a detachment of aircraft from VF-126 to make the training as realistic as possible. In March 1978, VF-126 received A-4F aircraft to improve the squadron's adversary support mission. In December 1980, the squadron began the first Turnaround ACM Programme (TAP) under which each fighter squadron participates in a dedicated two-week ACM improvement exercise that includes lectures and one-on-one sorties for each fighter aircrew. Dissimilar Air Combat Training (DACT) follows to provide experience in dealing with more than one adversary, each of whom could be flying a differnt type of aircraft, requiring a different response (in Vietnam, American fighters often encountered mixed bags of MiG-17, -19 and -21 aircraft). VF-126 operates three A-4Fs, 11 TA-4Js and three T-2Cs to perform the various functions of its mission.

ACM has definitely worked for the US Navy. Prior to the establishment of 'Top Gun' during the Vietnam War, 'US Navy flyers were scoring aerial kills at something less than a three-to-one ratio over the enemy . . . by the end of the war, Navy aircrews had mastered a 12.5 to 1 ratio over the adversary.' During this training, the A-4 – nicknamed the 'Mongoose' for its small size and stealth – has proven to be an ideal friendly adversary in ACM exercises throughout the Fleet.

Determined not to be caught short, as it was during the early stage of the Vietnam War, the Navy has expanded the ACM programme beyond 'Top Gun'. In 1974 the 'Royal Blues' of VA-127 were brought into the adversary programme to work with other light attack squadrons that would be prime targets of enemy fighting aircraft.

Commander R.L.Grant, commanding officer of the A-7 Corsair II squadron VA-122 noted that such training was needed to fill an ACM void that existed in light attack squadrons : 'In future conflicts, our forces will probably not enjoy the decisive air superiority prevalent in the Vietnam War . . . Incorrect procedures and bad habits are unconsciously developed from training only against other A-7 aircraft. It takes an encounter with dissimilar aircraft to identify training deficiencies.'

Hence, once again, the versatile A-4E was chosen to represent the adversary aircraft to disrupt the 'alpha' strikes that A-7s normally perform. A typical mission, led by Lieutenant-Commander Rocco Walker, then VA-127's assistant operations officer, against A-7Es of the 'Stingers' of VA-113 would go as follows :

'It is midday and wisps of cloud rise above the peaks. It is as if the mountains had drawn a deep breath and expelled the clouds into the air. They form a sort of fence inside which Rocco and the "Stingers" will go to work . . .

"Detaching !" says Stinger lead, Lieutenant George Cairnes. With him in the second Corsair is Lieutenant (junior grade) Paul Jorgenson. They dip down and away to set up for a run down the hall. Rocco stays high to loiter . . .

'Several miles out of view from Rocco, the A-7s start down the valley. Theoretically they carry ordnance and are inbound to a target. Rocco knows roughly where the

LEFT
The first A-4M (BuNo 158148) was similar in appearance to its predecessor, the A-4F, except, for the squared-off fin.

BELOW
Well-organized instrument lay-out in the A-4M cockpit is typical of the steady improvements in the Skyhawk programme over the years

A mixed bag of aircraft and weapons is seen in this view of (from left) a TA-4J of VMAT-102 with LAU-10A Zuni rocket launchers, an A-4M of VMA-142 (tail code MB), an A-4M of VMA-223 (tail code WP) carrying Paveway laser-guided bombs, and an A-4M of VMA-133 (tail code ME) also with Paveway LGBs

WP
0039
MARINES
ME
4987
MARINES
01

Corsairs are and the A-7s are aware than an enemy fighter could pounce on them at any time.

'A moment or so passes. In the cockpits, heads are on swivels, eyes dart up and down the horizon. Rocco sights a movement low at his ten o'clock position. "There they be," he says to himself, holding a shallow turn, patient.

'In defensive cruise formation – several hundred feet from each other – George and Paul search the sky. The butterflies have begun to squirm in their bellies.

"With a sudden but smooth movement, Rocco rolls and pulls his A-4 down through the horizon. His line of sight changes from sky blue to a blur of earth bronze. Against this panorama he eyes the glinting figures of the A-7s. He becomes a diving dart, aimed at the unsuspecting A-7s, gathering speed, 400 knots and increasing.

'From the trail A-7, a quick, clear voice : "Nine o'clock high, break left !"

ABOVE
Later production models of the A-4M, such as this aircraft assigned to VMA-223, had a fin-tip ECM antenna housing, as well as a 'chin-mounted' ECM recording and suppression aerial under the nose. Paveway LGBs are also loaded

RIGHT
A flight of new A-4Ms of the 'Blacksheep' VMA-214 on a formation training exercise over California

'One second, maybe two, of silence.

"Got 'em," says George in the lead, nearly grunting as he hauls his jet into a swift 4g turn.

'Rocco : "I'm engaged."

'The A-7s are bending around. Rocco bends with them in his dive, keeping the Corsairs on his nose as best he can. The airplanes cross well away from each other. Rocco pulls up, reversing.

"He's coming around !"

"Rog."

'The A-7s do a high-g one-eighty (180-degree turn).

'Was Rocco close enough in his run to send a missile or fire the cannons into the attackers ? In the terse seconds of eyeball-to-airplane contact could he have knocked an A-7 out of the sky ? Or were the Corsairs quick enough to evade ? That will be discussed later in the debrief on the ground.

'Meanwhile, the Corsairs pull and turn through the sky. Rocco chases. George and Paul try to avoid the pursuit. As the number two man, Paul has to keep George in sight, all the while trying to track Rocco. It's demanding work. George has to do essentially the same, relying on Paul to keep his safe distance.

'Rocco arcs to the east, zoom climbing. He is pressed into his seat by the gravitational forces. The Corsairs return to their base heading.

'Paul : "Still got him ?"

'George : "Affirm, he's high eastbound."

'Rocco intervenes : "OK, Stinger, good show. Let's disengage . . . and do it again."

There is, of course, no intent to turn light attack pilots into fighter pilots, but the heavy emphasis on ACM – and use of adversary squadrons – will surely prepare both attack and fighter pilots for circumstances in unprotected

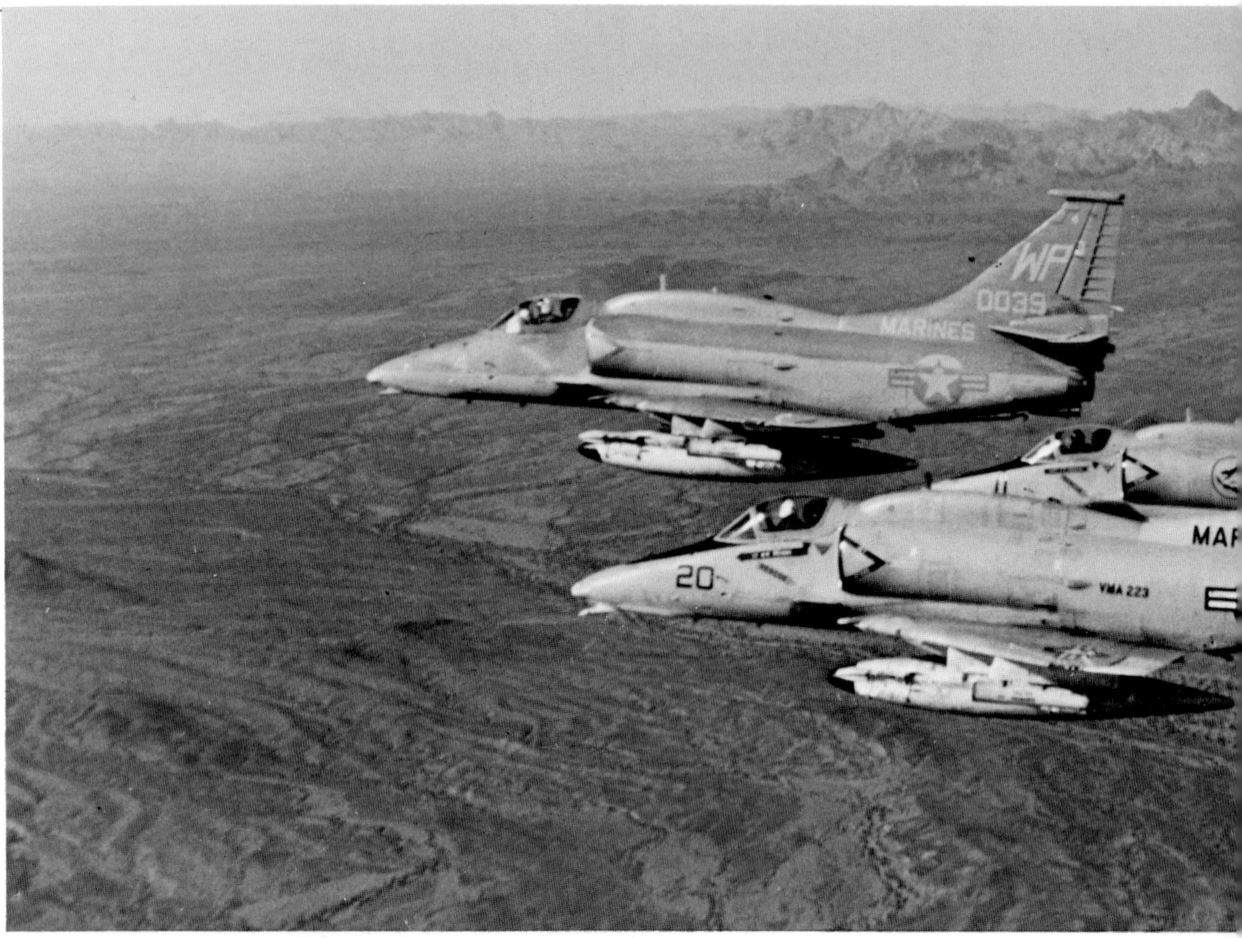
WP
0039
MARINES
20
VMA 223

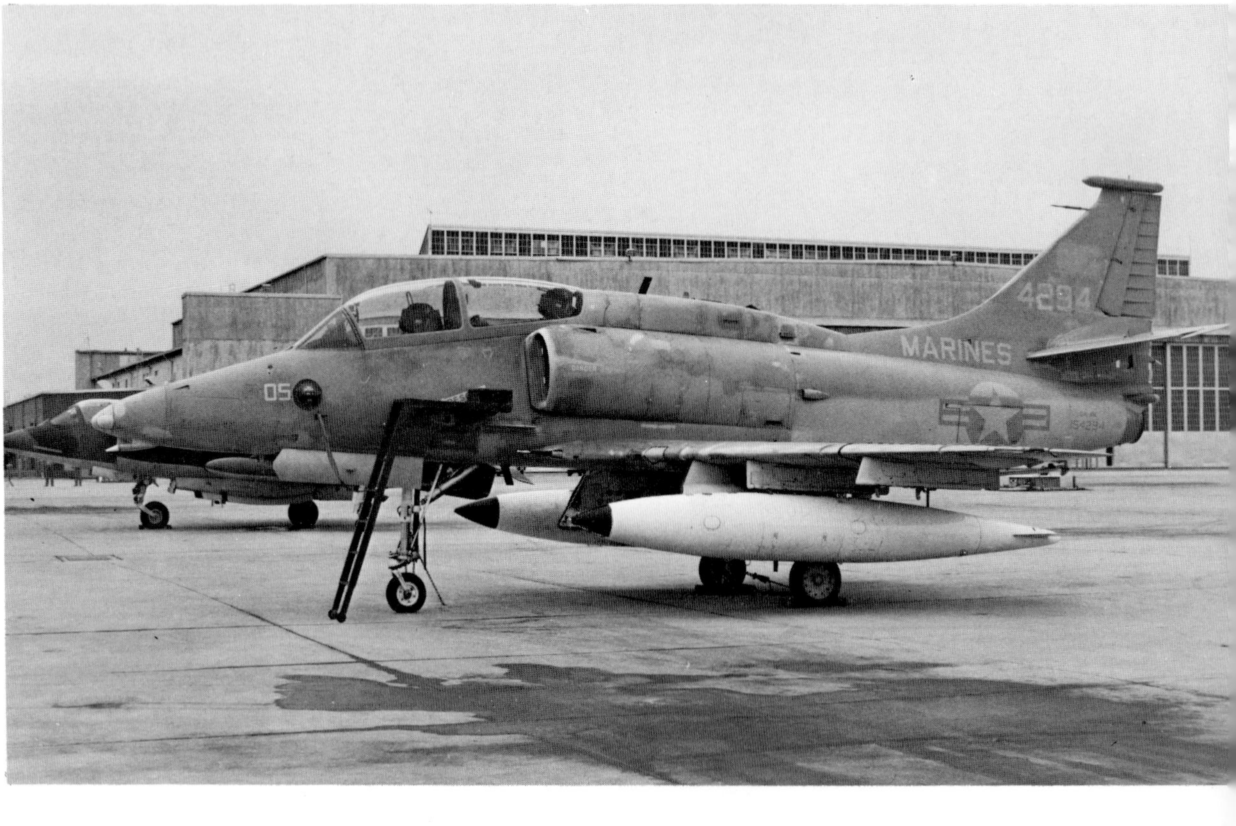
4294
MARINES
05

LEFT
An A-4M of VMA-223 (tail code WP) painted in the latest two-tone grey camouflage is followed, in formation, by another VMA-223 A-4M and an A-4M of VMA-221 (tail code CF) both finished in their squadron's highly visible colours

Below are two views of the latest Skyhawk development, the OA-4M forward air control version derived from the TA-4J. The various A-4M ECM antennae and avionics dorsal fairing have been fitted to the TA-4J airframe. This aircraft (BuNo 154294) is assigned to headquarters and maintenance squadron H&MS-32 at MCAS Cherry Point, North Carolina

ABOVE
Two A-4Fs in non-military markings were used in 1982 tests of Fairchild Republic Company's in-flight refuelling system pod, mounted on the center station of the lead aircraft. The FRC refuelling design uses a unique axial hose reel drive that offers operational simplicity and uses 25 percent fewer parts than earlier transverse reel pod. The new pod transfers at the rate of up to 450 (US) gallons per minute

RIGHT
Progressing to a single seat A-4M, a pilot with VMAT-102 drops 500-lb Snakeye retarded bombs ; the fins, opening after release, delay arrival on the target and allow the pilot time to clear the blast zone

air space. Given the flexibility of the A-4, it is sure to have a prominent role in ACM for some time to come.

The Blue Angels

The US Navy Flight Demonstration Squadron, more popularly known as the 'Blue Angels', has operated a number of high-performance aircraft since it was established in 1946. The squadron (or team, as it was originally described) use a succession of fighter aircraft – Grumman F6F Hellcat, F8F Bearcat, F9F-2 Panther, F9F-8 Cougar, F11F-1 Tiger and McDonnell F-4J Phantom II – before switching to the somewhat slower but more efficient A-4F in December 1973. What the new Blue Angles aircraft lost in speed from its twin-engined supersonic Phantoms was more than matched in the manoeuvrability of its new Skyhawks.

The specially modified A-4F used by the Navy Flight Demonstration Squadron is described by Lieutenant Scott Anderson, who currently flies the Number Three aircraft with the Blue Angels.

'The decision to use the A-4 was the result of increasing inflation and the skyrocketing cost of fuel, as well as the need for the aircraft that was easy to maintain. The A-4F Skyhawk is just what the Blue Angels needed. The A-4's tight turning radius, high thrust-to-weight ratio and roll rate of 720 degrees per second make it a natural for flight demonstration – especially for the squadron's solo pilots, who demonstrate the aircraft's maximum performance capabilities, in which the A-4's high roll rate and immediate power response are absolutely essential.'

The A-4Fs flown by the Blue Angels are visually distinctive by the lack of the dorsal avionics housing (not needed in this non-combat use of the aircraft). The aircraft have also had their weapons systems removed to enhance further the 'lean and clean' qualities so necessary for air show performances. These modifications significantly contribute to the squadron's overall performance, as noted by Lieutenant Anderson.

'Our aircraft are powered by the Pratt & Whitney J52-P-408 engine, which produces over 11,200lbs of thrust. With the aircraft weight at 11,400lbs, therefore, approximately halfway through an airshow demonstration the thrust-to-weight ratio of the aircraft is slightly less than 1 : 1.

'Our A-4s also have an inverted fuel system, which allows the aircraft to fly inverted for an extended length of time. Another unique modification is the Blue Angels' smoke-producing system. It is composed of a 30-gallon reservoir of a light-weight biodegradable paraffin-based oil which is pressurised by bleed air from the engine. The oil is then sprayed out of a small tube near the exhaust pipe of the aircraft, where hot exhaust gases transform the oil into smoke. the entire system is activated by the pilot, using a small switch on the throttle lever.

'The low number of man-hours required to keep an A-4 in tip-top condition is another big advantage of the A-4. During a two-week deployment, only 27 Blue Angels

MARINES
VMAT-102
21

NAVY/MARINES
DANGER
RESCUE

maintenance personnel are required to support the squadron's six A-4Fs, one TA-4J and one Lockheed C-130 Hercules support aircraft. It is indeed a tribute to the A-4 Skyhawk that the Blue Angels have successfully flown between 70 and 80 airshows a year for the last nine years in an aircraft that was developed nearly 30 years ago.

'For pilots trained in the high technology environment of the late 1970s and early 1980s, the A-4 is a pleasure to fly. Its small size, amazing power and outstanding manoeuvrability have made it a favourite of mine. It is probably one of the simplest aircraft around today, yet it is still the most popular adversary aircraft for training flight crews in air combat manoeuvring. The cockpit is extremely small, but once adjusted – even with my six-foot five-inch frame – it offers a tight, solid feeling similar to wearing a glove.

'All of the necessary system switches are readily available and the instruments are situated in such a way as to establish a very comfortable pilot scan. The A-4s flown by the Blue Angels have a much shorter control stick that allows the pilot to brace his right arm on his knee when flying, which is especially desirable when seeking a stable platform in close formation. The aircraft harness molds the pilot to the ejection seat through an inverted restraint system that holds him into the seat, even in negative *g* flight. The A-4F is easy to fly inverted and is extremely stable in that regime.'

Lieutenant Anderson had extensive experience in the A-7E Corsair prior to joining the Blue Angels in 1981. He trained with VA-174 (and later returned to that squadron as an instructor pilot and Training Landing Signal Officer). A graduate of the US Naval Academy, Anderson made two Mediterranean deployments with VA-83 aboard USS *Forrestal* (CV-59) and has more than 1,600 flight hours and 300 carrier landings to his credit.

With those credentials, Anderson's comments on the A-4 are of particular interest : 'Flying the same aircraft for 330 days out of the year creates an amazingly close relationship between the pilot and the plane. As for myself, I have more respect for the A-4F Skyhawk than I've ever had for any other piece of machinery.'

Forward Air Control

Inevitably, development of A-4 models also affects the TA-4 series. The most recent new use of the two-seat Skyhawk is as the OA-4M tactical control aircraft developed for the US Marine Corps. In this role, the second seat is occupied by a Forward Air Controller closely linked to the Marines' ground attack forces.

The first OA-4M was flown in June 1978. Since then, 23 Marine TA-4Fs have been converted to OA-4Ms by the Naval Air Rework Facility in Pensacola, Florida. Improvements in the OA-4M include : new ARC-159 UHF air communications radio, VHF radio for ground

The last production Skyhawk, an A-4M (BuNo 160264), on a demonstration flight displaying the flags of all the nations that have operated the aircraft

Four TA-4J's from VT-25 training squadron, flying in precise echelon port formation

communications, ARN-118 TACAN, ALQ-126 electronic counter-measures equipment, KY-28 secure voice system and ARL-45/50 radar warning system. The OA-4M is distinctive in appearance, having the dorsal avionics 'hump' and nose and tail ECM caps.

One of the units presently operating this 'new' Skyhawk is H&MS-32, which flies six OA-4Ms out of the MCAS Cherry Point, North Carolina. The Commanding Officer of H&MS-32, Colonel M.D.Ashworth, notes the present use of the aircraft:

'What do you get when you combine the present-day military needs for a fast airborne Forward Air Controller with the TA-4F? The OA-4M. Even though the idea of the "FastFAC" is not new, as evidenced by the use of the TA-4 in Vietnam, only recent has there been enough interest to develop a new role for this new version of the A-4.

'In a nutshell, the role of the OA-4M is to direct friendly air and naval gunfire and artillery in a manner that assures total target destruction. Through the use of the onboard radios, we have instant communication with the ground commander and give him immediate access to an arsenal of weapons that helps him best to employ his ground forces in a combat arena.

'Target acquisition is by no means a simple task and part of the role consists of choosing and marking the target with onboard rockets, through the use of other aircraft, or by directing artillery, naval gunfire or mortars. This utilises the entire array of OA-4M assets to complete the mission of the Forward Air Controller (Airborne)/Tactical Air Controller (Airborne).'

With the operational success already achieved by the OA-4Ms, it is reasonably certain that this variant will continue, in Marine Corps service for some time to come. Further, like the TA-4S used by Singapore in a dual training/close air support role, the OA-4M could well presage renewed interest in the two-seat Skyhawk.

The A-4 of Tomorrow

Clearly, the A-4 Skyhawk series will be a part of the world aviation scene for the next few decades. The A-4 of the future will not look much different from the aircraft now in service, although the aircraft has proven to be so adaptable that almost anything is possible. A good indication of the future worth of the A-4 can be seen in long-range Israeli plans for their aircraft: 'Significant reductions in the active A-4 inventory are expected throughout the late 1980s because of anticpated sales, attrition and storage. It is estimated that only one squadron of A-4 aircraft will remain by 1995 as an operational training unit.'

At that point, the A-4s – Israel and in several nations – will be rendering good service to pilots born long after the aircraft left El Segundo. An interesting tribute to what Ed Heinemann modestly referred to as 'just an honest, low-cost attack aeroplane that did better than it was intended.'

Citations

Medal of Honor

The Medal of Honour is the highest military decoration for bravery awarded to any individual in the armed forces of the United States of America. First awarded on 25 March 1863, this Medal has come to symbolise the highest standard of service far above and beyond the call of duty. Following the Vietnam War, it was bestowed on one Skyhawk pilot, as noted in the citation that accompanied the award:

Captain Michael J. Estocin, USN (posthumously)

'For conspicuous gallantry and intrepidity at the risk of his life above and beyond the call of duty on 20 and 26 April 1967 as a pilot in VA–192 embarked in USS *Ticonderoga* (CVA–14). Leading a three-plane group of aircraft in support of a coordinated strike against two thermal power plants in Haiphong, North Vietnam, on 20 April 1967, Captain (then Lieutenant-Commander) Estocin provided continuous warnings to the strike group leaders of the surface-to-air missile (SAM) threats, and personally neutralised three SAM sites. Although his aircraft was severely damaged by an exploding missile, he re-entered the target area and relentlessly prosecuted a Shrike attack in the face of intense anti-aircraft fire. With less than five minutes of fuel remaining he departed the target area and commenced inflight refueling which continued for over 100 miles. Three miles aft of *Ticonderoga,* and without enough fuel for a second approach, he disengaged from the tanker and executed a precise approach to a fiery arrested landing. On 26 April 1967, in the support of a coordinated strike against the vital fuel facilities in Haiphong, he led an attack on a threatening SAM site, during which his aircraft was seriously damaged by an exploding SAM; nevertheless, he regained control of his burning aircraft and courageously launched his Shrike missiles before departing the area. By his inspiring courage and unswerving devotion to duty in the face of grave personal danger, Captain Estocin upheld the highest traditions of the United States Naval Service.'

Navy Cross

The Navy Cross was established in February 1919 to honour members of the service who distinguished themselves by extraordinary heroism or distinguished service in the line of duty. The US Army's Distinguished Service Cross and the USAF's Air Force Cross are equivalents, all ranking just after the Medal of Honor.

During the Vietnam War, the Navy Cross was awarded to Skyhawk pilots as noted in the following citations:

Commander James R. Busey IV, USN

'For extraordinary heroism on 21 August 1967 as a pilot in VA–163, embarked in USS *Oriskany* (CVA–34). During a combat mission over North Vietnam, Commander (then Lieutenant-Commander) Busey was the leader of a section in a six-aircraft bombing element which attacked the Hanoi thermal power plant in the face of the enemy's most sophisticated and complex arsenal of air defence weapons. As he commenced his attack, Commander Busey sustained anti-aircraft hits to his aircraft. He skilfully regained control of his aircraft and, although his plane was severely damaged, renewed his attack, placing his weapons precisely on target. Subsequent bomb damage assessment photography confirmed that he inflicted heavy damage to his assigned portion of the thermal power plant. Although still severely handicapped by his damaged aircraft, Commander Busey evaded four surface-to-air missiles during his egress from the target area. Then, through skilful airmanship, he returned his crippled aircraft to the aircraft carrier. By his tenacious aggressiveness, professionalism, and heroic actions in the face of the enemy's massed and determined defences, Commander Busey upheld the highest traditions of the United States Naval Service.'

Commander Bryan W. Compton Jr, USN

'For extraordinary heroism as a pilot and as Commanding Officer of VA-163, embarked in USS *Oriskany* (CVA-34), on 21 August 1967. As the strike leader of a major coordinated air attack against the Hanoi Thermal Power Plant, Hanoi, North Vietnam, Commander Compton, with precise navigation and timing, led the strike group to the target area through an extremely intense array of sophisticated enemy defences, including at least 28 surface-to-air missiles and heavy, accurate anti-aircraft fire. Despite the continuing heavy enemy opposition in the target area, Commander Compton skilfully manoeuvred his strike forces and led them in an attack which inflicted major damage upon the target. During the attack, strike aircraft incurred extensive battle damage from the heavy flak opposition. With complete disregard for his own safety, Commander Compton remained in the vicinity of the target until the damaged aircraft exited the area safely. In addition to assisting the egressing strike pilots by calling evasive manoeuvres necessary for them to avoid surface-to-air missiles and heavy concentrations of anti-aircraft artillery fire, he succeeded in taking 17 pictures with a hand-held camera which provided immediate and invaluable damage assessment of this most significant target. By his superb leadership, outstanding courage and inspiring devotion to duty in the face of extremely heavy enemy opposition, Commander Compton contributed greatly to the success of a most hazardous mission and upheld the highest traditions of the United States Naval Service.'

Lieutenant Edward A. Dickson, USNR (posthumously)

'For extraordinary heroism on 7 February 1965 while serving as a jet attack pilot with VA-155 aboard the USS *Coral Sea* (CVA-43), during a retaliatory air strike against the Dong Hoi Army Barracks and staging area in North Vietnam. When his aircraft was struck by intense enemy anti-aircraft fire on a low-level run-in to the target area and burst into flames, Lieutenant Dickson elected to remain with his burning plane until he had released his bombs on the target area. Following his attack, he headed toward the sea where he ejected from his flaming aircraft. By his inspiring and courageous devotion to duty, Lieutenant Dickson upheld the finest traditions of the United States Naval Service.'

Captain Trent R. Powers, USN (posthumously)

'For extraordinary heroism on 31 October 1965 while serving as a pilot of jet attack aircraft with VA-164, embarked in USS *Oriskany* (CVA-34), during a combat mission over hostile territory in North Vietnam. Captain (then Lieutenant-Commander) Powers was assigned the demanding and unusual task of leading a two-division, United States Air Force flight into an an area heavily defended by anti-aircraft artillery and surface-to-air missiles, with the mission of locating and destroying the missile installations. He planned the attack route and led the eight-plane group over more than 600 miles of unfamiliar, cloud-shrouded mountainous terrain, arriving in the target area precisely at a pre-briefed time that has been selected to coincide with the strikes of two carrier air wings against a bridge. The target area was the scene of an intense air-to-ground battle, many surface-to-air missiles were being fired and heavy enemy anti-aircraft fire was observed in all directions. With full knowledge of the serious hazards involved, Captain Powers courageously led the Air Force aircraft into battle. His bombs and those of the Air Force aircraft which he had led inflicted severe damage to both missile sites. By his superior aeronautical skill and valiant determination, Captain Powers upheld the highest traditions of the United States Naval Service.'

Lieutenant-Commander Marvin D. Reynolds, USN

'For extraordinary heroism on 17 July 1967 as a pilot in VA–163, embarked in USS *Oriskany* (CVA–34). As the leader of a section of A–4E aircraft conducting a search and rescue mission for a pilot downed the previous day*, 32 miles southwest of Hanoi, North Vietnam, Lieutenant-Commander Reynolds proceeded 70 miles inland through darkness and heavy anti-aircraft artillery fire to the search area where he succeeded in establishing contact with the downed pilot. When the Search and Rescue Commander informed him that positive voice contact with the pilot must be established before the helicopter could cross the beach, Lieutenant-Commander Reynolds re-entered the area and established voice contact. Due to his low fuel state, he was forced to aerial refuel before returning to the scene, this time leading the rescue forces. Manoeuvring so as to evade three surface-to-air missile launchings, he led the flight to the rescue scene. He attacked and silenced a large flak site endangering the helicopter. Lieutenant-Commander Reynolds then made repeated, dangerously low passes over the pilot to ensure a successful pickup. During egress, he successfully attacked and silenced one of the most menacing flak sites on the helicopter's egress route. By his courageous conduct, exceptional skill, and fearless devotion to duty, he was primarily responsible for the successful rescue of the downed pilot, thereby upholding the finest traditions of the United States Naval Service.'

Commander Burton H. Shepherd, USN

'For extraordinary heroism in aerial flight on 26 October 1967 as Commander, Attack Carrier Air Wing 16, embarked in USS *Oriskany* (CVA–34). As the strike leader of an 18-plane strike group launched against the strategically located and heavily defended Hanoi thermal power plant in North Vietnam, Commander Shepherd, although hampered by adverse weather conditions en route, maintained the precise timing necessay to execute properly the intricate strike plan. Skilfully manoeuvring to avoid the numerous tracking missiles and intense and accurate barrages of 57-mm and 85-mm flak, he led the strike group to the optimum roll-in point and then aggressively pressed home his attack, releasing all bombs on target. Egressing from the target area in a hail of enemy fire, he retired to the relative safety of the Karst hills and checked in his strike group. After proceeding expeditiously to the coast to refuel, Commander Shepherd returned to an area south of the target to search for one of his missing strike pilots. Continuing the search for more than an hour over enemy terrain in the face of the most concentrate enemy fire in North Vietnam, he finally returned to the coast after reaching a low fuel state. By his aggressive leadership, professional airmanship, and determination, Commander Shepherd contributed in large measure to the destruction of this major target, and upheld the highest traditions of the United States Naval Service.'

Captain Homer L. Smith, USN (posthumously)

'For extraordinary heroism on 19 and 20 May 1967, while serving as Commanding Officer of VA–212, embarked in USS *Bonn Homme Richard* (CVA–31), during aerial attacks on two strategically important and heavily defended thermal power plants in Hanoi and Bac Giang, North Vietnam. As strike leader in each of these actions against the enemy, Captain (then Commander) Smith was faced with adverse weather and difficult terrain, formidable opposition from the enemy, and the necessity for violent, evasive manoeuvring. Despite these obstacles, he expertly led his strike groups in executing brilliantly successful attacks which substantially hindered the enemy in his efforts to make war. By his heroic actions, superb airmanship, and inspiring devotion to duty throughout, Captain Smith reflected great credit upon himself and his squadron, and upheld the highest traditions of the United States Naval Service.'

*Lieutenant-Commander Demetrio 'Butch' Verich, pilot of an LTV F–8E Crusader of VF–162, also deployed aboard USS *Oriskany*.

Technical & Production Data

compiled by Harry S. Gann

26 July 1952	Preliminary design begins
13 October 1952	Authority to proceed
22 June 1954	First flight – R. O. Rahn
October 1954	Authority to proceed A4D-2
14 October 1955	A4D-1 set World's Speed Record for 500 kilometer closed course – 695.163 mph
26 March 1956	First flight A4D-2
November 1956	First factory-to-fleet delivery A4D-1
January 1957	First operational USMC Squadron
September 1957	Authority to proceed A4D-2N
21 August 1958	First flight A4D-2N
15 April 1960	Authority to proceed A-4G for Australia
May 1960	Authority to proceed A-4E
12 July 1961	First flight A-4E
July 1964	Authority to proceed TA-4E
30 June 1965	First flight TA-4E
December 1965	Contract to modify A-4B to A-4P for Argentina
16 April 1966	Authority to proceed TA-4G for Australia
19 May 1966	First factory-to-fleet delivery TA-4(E)F
31 August 1966	First flight A-4F
10 October 1966	Authority to proceed A-4H for Israel
1 May 1967	A-4C shoots down MiG with Zuni Missile
19 July 1967	First flight A-4G
7 August 1967	First flight TA-4G
27 October 1967	First flight A-4H
26 February 1968	Authority to proceed TA-4H for Israel
3 July 1968	Authority to proceed A-4K and TA-4K for New Zealand
19 December 1968	Authority to proceed TA-4J
15 April 1969	First flight TA-4H
6 June 1969	First factory-to-fleet delivery TA-4J
21 August 1969	First flight A-4L
10 November 1969	First flight A-4K
5 December 1969	First flight TA-4K
10 April 1970	First flight A-4M
4 March 1971	Authority to proceed A-4N for Israel
8 June 1972	First flight A-4N
September 1973	A-4F selected for Blue Angels
10 January 1975	Authority to proceed A-4KU and TA-4KU for Kuwait
20 July 1976	First flight A-4KU
27 February 1979	Delivery last A-4, No. 2960

MODEL	AMOUNT	FROM	TO	REMARKS
XA4D-1	1		137812	Redesignated A4D-1
A4D-1/A-4A	19	137813	137831	
	52	139919	139970	
	94	142142	142235	
Subtotal	166			
A4D-2/A-4B	60	142082	142141	
	8	142416	142423	
	280	142674	142953	
	194	144868	145061	
Subtotal	542			
A4D-3	0	145147	145156	Cancelled
A4D-2N/A-4C	85	145062	145146	
	0	146460	146693	Cancelled
	181	147669	147849	
	14	148304	148317	
	178	148435	148612	
	160	149487	148646	
	20	150581	150600	
Subtotal	638			
A4D-5/A-4E	2	148613	148614	
	20	149647	149666	
	180	149959	150138	
	180	151022	151201	
	0	151202	151261	Cancelled
	118	151984	152101	152101 converted to Prototype A-4F
Subtotal	500			
A-4F	46	154172	154217	
	100	154970	155069	155042, 155049 converted to A-4M
Subtotal	146			
TA-4F	1	152102	152103	
	33	152846	152878	
	31	153660	153690	
	73	153459	153531	Most TA-4F converted to TA-4J
	57	154287	154343	(23) converted to OA-4M for USMC
	44	154614	154657	
	1		155071	
Subtotal	241			
A-4G	8	154903	154910	Plus 8 A-4F aircraft from U.S.N.
Subtotal	8			
TA-4G	2	154911	154912	Plus 2 TA-4F aircraft from U.S.N.
Subtotal	2			
A-4H	48	155242	155289	
	34	157395	157428	
	8	157918	157925	
Subtotal	90			
TA-4H	6	157429	157434	
	4	157926	157929	
Subtotal	10			
TA-4J	1		155070	
	48	155072	155119	
	60	156891	156950	
	75	158073	158147	
	75	158453	158527	
	12	158712	158723	
	6	159090	159104	
Subtotal	277			
TA-4J(H)	11	159546	159556	
	4	159795	159798	
Subtotal	15			

MODEL	AMOUNT	FROM	TO	REMARKS
A-4K	10	157904	157913	
Subtotal	10			
TA-4K	4	157914	157917	
Subtotal	4			
A-4L	(100)	Service Kits - From A-4C		
A-4M	49	158148	158196	
	24	158412	158435	
	20	159470	159489	
	4	159490	159493	
	13	159778	159790	
	24	160022	160045	
Subtotal	158			
A-4N	18	158726	158743	
	18	159035	159052	
	24	159075	159098	
	12	159515	159526	
	26	159799	159824	
	19	159527	159545	
Subtotal	117			
A-4P	(50)			A-4B Aircraft Modified for Argentine Air Force
A-4Q	(25)			A-4B Aircraft Modified for Argentine Navy
A-4S	(98)			A-4B/C Aircraft Modified for Singapore Air Force
TA-4S	(9)			A-4B/C Aircraft Modified for Singapore Air Force
A-4KU	30	160180	160209	Kuwait Air Force
TA-4KU	6	160210	160215	Kuwait Air Force
	(88)			to make 68 A-4L for Royal Malaysian Air Force
	(30)			A-4E/H for Indonesian Air Force, from Israel
	(2)			TA-4H for Indonesian Air Force, from Israel

GENERAL DATA

	A-4A	A-4B	A-4C	A-4E	A-4F	TA-4F	A-4K	A-4M	A-4N
WING SPAN	27'6"								
FUSELAGE LENGTH	38'4$\frac{3}{4}$"		39'1$\frac{3}{4}$"	40'3$\frac{1}{4}$"		42'7$\frac{1}{4}$"	40'3$\frac{1}{4}$"		
FUSELAGE HEIGHT	15'								
EMPTY WEIGHT	8,400lbs.	9,146	9,728	9,853	10,448	10,602	10,000	10,465	
MAXIMUM TAKE-OFF WEIGHT	20,000lbs.	22,500		24,500					
MAXIMUM LEVEL SPEED	664mph	661	649	673		675	673		
ENGINE	J65-W-4	J65-W-16A		J52-P-6A	J52-P8A	J52-P-6A	J52-P-8A	J52-P-408A	
THRUST (STATIC)	7,700lbs.		8,500	8,500	9,300	8,500	9,300	11,200	

MAIN DIFFERENCES TABLE

	A-4A	A-4B	A-4P ARG AF	A-4Q ARG NAVY	A-4C	A-4E	A-4F	TA-4F
ENGINE	J65-W16A	J65-W-16A J65-W-20	J-65-W-20	J-65-W-20	J-65-W-16A J65-W-20	J52-P-6A, 6B J52-P-8A, 8B	J52-P-8A, 8B J52-P-408	J52-P-6A, J52-P-8A,
THRUST (lbs)	7,700	7,700 8,400	8,400	8,400	7,700 8,400	8,500 9,300	9,300 11,200	8,500 9,300
FUSELAGE Fueling Probe Air Refueling Intake Ducts	NO NO FLUSH	YES YES FLUSH	YES NO FLUSH	YES NO FLUSH	YES YES FLUSH	YES YES SEPARATED	YES YES SEPARATED	YES YES SEPARAT
UPPER AVIONICS COMPARTMENT	NO	NO	NO	NO	NO	YES	YES	NO
AFCS	NO	NO	NO	NO	YES	YES	YES	YES
RADAR	NO	NO	NO	NO	AN/APG-53A	AN/APG-53A	AN/APG-53A	AN/APG-5
VIDEO IP-936/AXQ	NO	NO	NO	NO	NO	PROV. ONLY	PROV. ONLY	SOME
NAVIGATION COMPUTER	NONE	AN/ASN-19A	AN/ASN-19A	AN/ASN-19A	AN/ASN-19A	AN/ASN-19A (EARLY A-4E) AN/ASN-41	AN/ASN-41	AN/ASN-
LABS	AERO 18B	AERO 18B	NO	NO	AN/AJB-3	AN/AJB-3 AN/AJB-3A	AN/AJB-3A	AN/AJB-
CP-741/A	NO	NO	NO	NO	NO	YES	YES	YES
OXYGEN SYSTEM	5 LITRE	5 LITRE	5 LITRE	5 LITRE	10 LITRE	10 LITRE	10 LITRE	10 LITRE
EXTENDABLE CONTROL STICK	YES	YES	YES	YES	NO	NO	NO	NO
FUEL GUAGING Fuselage Wing Drop Tanks	1 PROBE 2 PROBE YES	1 PROBE 2 PROBE YES	1 PROBE 2 PROBE YES	1 PROBE 2 PROBE YES	1 PROBE 6 PROBE YES	1 PROBE 6 PROBE YES	1 PROBE 6 PROBE YES	1 PROBE 6 PROBE YES
FUSELAGE FUEL CELL CAPACITY	1600 lb	1600 lb	1600 lb	1600 lb	1600 lb	1600 lb	1600 lb	700 lb
ELEVATOR	BOOSTED	POWERED	POWERED	POWERED	POWERED	POWERED	POWERED	POWERE
AILERON POWER	SINGLE	TANDEM	TANDEM	TANDEM	TANDEM	TANDEM	TANDEM	TANDEI
STABILIZER TRIM 12 Degrees Noseup 1 Degree Nosedown 11 Degrees Noseup 1 Degree Nosedown 12-1/4 Degrees Noseup 1 Degree Nosedown	YES NO NO	NO YES NO	NO YES NO	NO YES NO	NO YES NO	NO NO YES	NO NO YES	NO YES NO
BOMB RACKS	3	3	3	3	3	5	5	5
ROCKET EJECTION SEAT	ESCAPC 1	ESCAPAC 1 STENCEL MOD	ESCAPAC 1 STENCEL MOD	ESCAPAC 1 STENCEL MOD	ESCAPAC 1 STENCEL MOD	ESCAPAC 1 STENCEL MOD	ESCAPAC 1C-3	ESCAPA 1C-3
NOSEWHEEL STEERING	NO	NO	NO	NO	NO	NO	YES	YES
SPOILERS	NO	NO	YES	YES	NO	NO†	YES	YES
DRAG CHUTE	NO	NO	NO	NO	NO	NO	NO	NO
COMMUNICATIONS	RT-355/ ASQ-17 (AN/ARC-27A)	RT-355/ ASQ-17 (AN/ARC-27A)	ARC-109 UHF 618M-2D VHF	ARC-109 UHF 618M-2D VHF	RT-355/ * ASQ-17 (AN/ARC-27A)	RT-355/ * ASQ-17 (AN-ARC-27A)	AN/ARC-51A AN/ARR-69	AN/ARC-5 AN/ARR-
RADAR IDENTIFICATION (IFF)	RT-354/ (AN/APX-6B) ASQ-17	RT-354/ (AN/APX-6B) ASQ-17	AN APX-72	AN APX-72	RT-354/ * (AN/APX-6B) ASQ-17	* RT-354/(AN/APX-6B) ASQ-17	AN/APX-64(V)	AN/APX-6
APC AN/ASN-54	NO	NO	NO	NO	YES	YES	YES	PROVISIO ONLY
DOPPLER AN/APN-153	NO	NO	NO	NO	NO	SOME	YES	YES
TACAN	AN/ARN-21D	AN/ARN-21D	AN/ARN-21D	AN/ARN-21D	AN/ARN-21D *	AN/ARN-21D * (EARLY A-4E) ARN-52(V)	AN/ARN-52(V)	AN/ARN-5
ADF	AM-1260/ ASQ-17 (AN-ARA-25)	AM-1260/ ASQ-17 (AN/ARA-25)	DFA-73	DF-203	AM-1260/ * ASQ-17 (AN/ARA-25)	AM-1260/ * ASQ-17 (AN/ARA-25)	AN/ARA-50	AN/ARA-
ILS	NO	NO	51RV-1	51RV-1	NO	NO	AN/ARA-63	NO
SELF STARTER	NO	NO	NO	NO	NO	NO	NO	NO
JATO	NO	NO	NO	NO	SOME PROVISIONS ONLY	SOME PROVISIONS ONLY	PARTIAL PROVISIONS	PARTIA PROVISIO
RADAR ALTIMETER	NO	AN APN-141	PROVISIONS ONLY	PROVISIONS ONLY	AN/APN-141	AN/APN-141	AN/APN-141	AN/APN-
AIMS	NO	NO	NO	NO	PROVISIONS * AFC-482	PROVISIONS * AFC-482	PARTIAL PROVISIONS	PARTIA PROVISIO
ECM	NO	NO	NO	NO	PROVISIONS ONLY	PROVISIONS ONLY	PROVISIONS ONLY	SOME
SPECIAL WEAPON	YES	YES	NO	NO	YES	YES	YES	YES
SIDEWINDER	NO	NO	PROVISIONS ONLY	PROVISIONS ONLY	SOME AFC-203A	NO	TWO STATION BY AFC	NO
BULLPUP	NO	PROVISIONS ONLY	NO	NO	PROVISIONS ONLY	PROVISIONS ONLY	PROVISIONS ONLY	PROVISIO ONLY
GCBS	NO	SOME PROVISIONS ONLY	NO	NO	PROVISIONS ONLY	PROVISIONS ONLY	PROVISIONS ONLY	PROVISIO ONLY
SHRIKE	NO	NO	NO	NO	LIMITED SHRIKE	YES	YES	YES
WALLEYE	NO	NO	NO	NO	NO	PROVISIONS ONLY	PROVISIONS ONLY	PROVISIO ONLY/SO
GUNS	20 MM 200 RDS	20MM 200RDS	20MM 200 RDS	20MM 200 RDS	20MM 200 RDS	20MM 200 RDS	20MM 200 RDS	20MM 200 RD
WDS & HUD	NO	NO	NO	NO	NO	NO	NO	NO

* AFC 482 UPDATES A-4C/E AVIONICS TO A-4F CONFIGURATIONS

† AFC 442 INC SPOILERS

A-4G	TA-4G	A-4H	TA-4H	TA-4J	A-4K	TA-4K	A-4L	A-4M	A-4N
-P-8A, 8B	J52-P-8A, 8B	J52-P-8A, 8B	J52-P-8A, 8B	J52-P-6A, 6B J52-P-8A, 8B	J52-P-8A, 8B	J52-P-8A, 8B	J65-W-20	J52-P-408	J52-P-408
,300	9,300	9,300	9,300	8,500 9,300	9,300	9,300	8,400	11,200	11,200
YES YES ARATED	YES YES SEPARATED	YES YES SEPARATED	YES YES SEPARATED	YES YES SEPARATED	YES YES SEPARATED	YES YES SEPARATED	YES YES FLUSH	YES YES SEPARATED	YES YES SEPARATED
VISIONS ONLY	NO	PROVISIONS ONLY	NO	NO	YES	NO	YES	YES	YES
YES	YES	YES	YES	YES	YES	YES	YES	YES	YES
APG-53A	AN/APG-53A	AN/APG-53A	AN/APG-53A	NO	AN/APG-53A	AN/APG-53A	AN/APG-53A	AN/APG-53A PROVISIONS ONLY	AN/APQ-145
NO	NO	NO	NO	NO	NO		PROV. ONLY	PROV. ONLY	PROV. ONLY
ASN-41	AN/ASN-41	AN/ASN-41	AN/ASN-41	PROV. ONLY	AN/ASN-41	AN/ASN-41	AN/ASN-19A	AN/ASN-41 PROVISIONS ONLY	AN/ASN-41
V. ONLY VIRING)	PROV. ONLY (WIRING)	PROV. ONLY (WIRING)	PROV. ONLY (WIRING)	PROV. ONLY (WIRING)	PROV. ONLY	PROV. ONLY	AN/AJB-3A	AN/AJB-3A	NO
NO	NO	NO	NO	PROV. ONLY	PROV. ONLY	PROV. ONLY	YES	YES	NO
LITRE	10 LITRE	HI PRESSURE GASEOUS	HI PRESSURE GASEOUS	10 LITRE	10 LITRE	10 LITRE	10 LITRE	10 LITRE	10 LITRE
NO	NO	NO	NO	NO	NO	NO	NO	NO	NO
PROBE PROBE YES	1 PROBE 6 PROBE YES	1 PROBE 6 PROBE YES	1 PROBE 6 PROBE YES	1 PROBE 6 PROBE YES	1 PROBE 6 PROBE YES	1 PROBE 6 PROBE YES	1 PROBE 6 PROBE YES	1 PROBE 6 PROBE YES	1 PROBE 6 PROBE YES
600 lb	700 lb	1600 lb	700 lb	700 lb	1600 lb	700 lb	1600 lb	1600 lb	1600 lb
WERED	POWERED	POWERED	POWERED	POWERED	POWERED	POWERED	POWERED	POWERED	POWERED
NDEM	TANDEM	TANDEM	TANDEM	TANDEM	TANDEM	TANDEM	TANDEM	TANDEM	TANDEM
NO NO YES	NO NO YES	NO NO YES	NO NO YES	NO NO YES	NO NO YES	NO NO YES	NO YES NO	NO NO YES	NO NO YES
5	5	5	5	5	5	5	3	5	5
CAPAC 1C-3	ESCAPAC 1C-3	ESCAPAC 1C-3	ESCAPAC 1C-3	ESCAPAC 1C-3 1F-3	ESCAPAC 1C-3	ESCAPAC 1C-3	ESCAPAC 1 STENCEL MOD	ESCAPAC 1C-3 1F-3	ESCAPAC 1C-3
YES	YES	YES	YES	YES	YES	YES	NO	YES	YES
YES	YES	YES	YES	YES	YES	YES	YES	YES	YES
NO	NO	YES	YES	NO	YES	YES	NO	YES	YES
ARC-51A ARR-69	AN/ARC 51A AN/ARR-69	DUAL AN/ARC-51A AN/ARR-69	DUAL AN/ARC 51A AN/ARR-69	AN/ARC-51A AN/ARR-69	AN/ARC-51A AN/ARC-115 (VHF-AM) AN/ARR-69	AN/ARC-51A AN/ARC-115 (VHF-AM) AN/ARR-69	AN/ARC-51A AN/ARR-69	AN/ARC-51A AN/ARR-69 AN/ARR-114 (VHF-FM)	DUAL AN/ARC-51A AN/ARR-69
PX-64(V)	AN/APX-64(V)	AN/APX-46	AN/APX-46	AN/APX-64(V) AN/APX-72	AN/APX-72(V)	AN/APX-72(V)	AN/APX-64(V)	AN/APX-72(V)	AN/APX-72(V)
NO	NO	NO	NO	PROVISIONS ONLY	NO	NO	YES	PROVISIONS ONLY	NO
YES	YES	YES	YES	PROVISIONS ONLY	YES	YES	NO	PROVISIONS ONLY	YES
RN-52(V)	AN/ARN-52(V)	NO	NO	AN/ARN-52(V) AN/ARN-84	AN/ARN-52(V)	AN/ARN-52(V)	AN/ARN 52(V)	AN/ARN-52(V) AN/ARN-84	NO
ARA-50	AN/ARA-50	AN/ARA-50	AN/ARA-50	AN/ARA-50	AN/ARA-50	AN/ARA-50	AN/ARA-50	AN/ARA-50	AN/ARA-50
NO	NO	NO	NO	NO	NO	NO	NO	NO	NO
NO	NO	NO	NO	NO	NO	NO	NO	YES	NO
RTIAL VISIONS	PARTIAL PROVISIONS	PARTIAL PROVISIONS	PARTIAL PROVISIONS	PARTIAL PROVISIONS	PARTIAL PROVISIONS	PARTIAL PROVISIONS	SOME PROVISIONS ONLY	COMPLETE PROVISIONS	PARTIAL PROVISIONS
APN-411	AN/APN-141	AP/APN-141	AN/APN-141	AN/APN-141	AN/APN-141	AN/APN-141	AN/APN-141	AN/APN-141 AN/APN-194	AN/APN-194
NO	NO	NO	NO	PARTIAL PROVISIONS	NO	NO	PROVISIONS AFC-482	PROVISIONS ONLY	PROVISIONS EXCEPT KIT/T SEC
NO	NO	NO	NO	NO	PROVISIONS ONLY	NO	PROVISIONS ONLY	PROVISIONS ONLY	PROVISIONS ONLY
NO	NO	NO	NO	NO	NO	NO	YES	YES	NO
OUR ATION	FOUR STATION	FOUR STATIONS	FOUR STATIONS	NO	TWO STATIONS	NO	SOME AFC-203A	NO	FOUR STATIONS
VISIONS NLY	PROVISIONS ONLY	NO	NO	NO	PROVISIONS ONLY	PROVISIONS ONLY	PROVISIONS ONLY	PROVISIONS ONLY	PROVISIONS ONLY
NO	NO	NO	NO	NO	NO	NO	PROVISIONS ONLY	YES	NO
NO	NO	NO	NO	PROVISIONS ONLY	PROVISIONS ONLY	PROVISIONS ONLY	YES	YES	YES
NO	NO	NO	NO	NO	NO	NO	PROVISIONS ONLY	PROVISIONS ONLY	YES
MM RDS	20MM 200 RDS	20MM 200RDS 30MM 300RDS	20MM 200 RDS	20MM 200 RDS	20MM 200 RDS	20MM 200 RDS	20MM 200 RDS	20MM 400 RDS	30MM 300 RDS
NO	NO	NO	NO	NO	NO	NO	NO	NO	YES

Index